CREATION SONGS

INTERPRETATIONS OF THE PSALMS

by

JOHN LESTER YOUNG

Designer: Emily J. Green

To order additional copies of this book, contact:
Xlibris
844-714-8691
www.Xlibris.com
Orders@Xlibris.com

ISBN: Softcover   978-1-4134-5132-0
         Hardcover   978-1-4134-5133-7

Library of Congress Control Number: 2004091750

Print information available on the last page

Rev. date: 12/10/2021

INTRODUCTION

In Greek, the word psalm means the twanging of the harp. Psalms are poetry meant not only to convey religious meaning but spiritual music, not only holy depths but joyful rhythms. For Jews and Christians, the book of Psalms has been a central foundation for their worship throughout their histories. Its poetry is probably the best known and most used poetry in the world. Few Jewish or Christian worship services have been without a reference to the Psalms. Countless individuals use phrases from the Psalms almost every day.

Traditionally, these 150 or so songs were thought to have been written by King David about 1000 years before Jesus lived. In fact, elements from the Book of Psalms have been discovered in earlier cultures. Long before the Jews were a kingdom, psalms were being written and sung in the Middle East, and the Jews learned much of their style and some of the substance for their Psalms from the Canaanites, Babylonians, and other ancient civilizations. However, the Jews put into the Book of Psalms their unique vision of God and life, and consolidated the Psalms, as we know them, about the time King David ruled. Scholars think it is unlikely that King David wrote many of the Psalms personally, but certainly his spirit affected their style and content, as much or more than King James of England shaped his well-known version of the Bible. Christians have added their spirit and passion to the wealth of the Psalms throughout the two thousand years of their evolution. Western literary and philosophical history is awash with thinkers and activists making the Psalms their own. Millions of individual people throughout the world have rested in the embrace of these verses.

How do we make the best use of the Psalms? They were written three thousand years ago and have since been reshaped, translated, and re-interpreted innumerable times. The Psalms often have a tribal feel, are full of laments about ancient conflicts, celebrations of kingly struggles, and the prayerful rituals of ancient priests in Jerusalem. Many of the details are in language, style, and content from the original Hebrew texts that remain a mystery even to the most informed contemporary scholars. While the Psalms are a foundation of our Jewish and Christian faiths, and have been the basis for Western worship, I felt, as a young person, that many of them were almost sacrilegious, not gracious but complaining, not grateful but full of rage, not loving but seeking revenge.

A passion grew in me to become so at home with the Psalms that I could interpret each of these songs in ways that made sense as spiritual gifts from my ancient religious ancestors. I have done this over many years. I have done my best to treat each of the Psalms with integrity, and to put the integrity I found into words that conveyed spiritual truth and beauty. I have grown much in the course of this blessed ordeal. The Psalms are still a treasure trove for the spiritual seeker, and a surprising catalyst for the millions of faithful. My interpretations are intended to be accessible to Jews and to Christians, to believers and to non-believers, to the faithful and to the seeker. Because the Psalms for me are larger than Judaism or Christianity alone, I have added twenty-six photos that connect our whole world with the verses in the Psalms.

I hope that *Creation Songs: Interpretations of the Psalms* will help many of my contemporaries to make the Psalms their own, to find their personal truths in the words of the Psalms, and to heal their spirits in these ancient poems. I hope, as you look at and consider *Creation Songs* that you, too, will be empowered not only to discover religious meaning but spiritual music, not only to feel others' spiritual depths, but to rediscover and to savor the joyful rhythms of your own souls. For each of us is a living tradition; so, twang the harps of life until they sing.

ONE

Help us not to walk in the counsel of the unjust,
Nor to eat from the table of the corrupted,
Nor to sit in the seat of the scornful.
Let our delight be in the laws of love.
May we live these laws day and night.

Then, like trees planted by flowing rivers,
Bringing forth good harvests,
Our leaves may not wither before their time,
And what we do will help the world to prosper.

For the unjust, it is not so.
They are like chaff which the wind drives away.
The unjust will not endure even their own judgments;
Nor risk remaining members of any congregation seeking truth.
The just will find a way to truth,
While the unjust lose themselves in emptiness.

Cherry blossoms and water:
Branch Brook Park, Newark, New Jersey

TWO

Vanity is a strange rage.
The well-born set themselves apart;
The powerful take counsel together,
Both against the good of the Earth
And the wishes of the common people.
The vain try to break the hold of nature's magnificent balance.
They cast away their community with humanity.

How the heavens must laugh;
What objects of derision we must be in the eyes of cosmic justice.
For by the standards of nature and love,
How often our anger should be fear.

Yet, the hills rise in their splendor,
And the world has chosen all of us to be its children.
We are given life.
Even the frontiers of the Earth are our home.

Anger, so often, breaks down into frustration and failure.
Possession usually contains only emptiness.
Be wise, and learn the lessons of nature and of love,
For we are judges in the Earth.

Serve the Earth with wonder and the people with respect.
Both are worthy of fear, for all power is ultimately theirs.
Embrace them with your deeds, and put your trust in their strength.

THREE

Creator, criticism troubles me;
Condemnation takes my energy away and burdens my spirit.
When anyone gives up and judges me:
'Beyond changing for the better,'
They have taken on a god's mantle.
They make ultimate judgments in their condemnations.

Life has not so judged me.
I live, breathe, and see the beauty of the Earth.
Life blesses me with sleep, morning, and the light of the Sun.

I shall not be afraid, even of many critics.
Help me to listen, to learn, and to change for the better.
But may only truth be spoken and heard;
May changes be simply for courage and for compassion's sake.

Like condemnation, salvation is a cosmic gesture.
Life is your salvation for each of us.
I am grateful for your peace, for your faith in me.

FOUR

God, you are my righteousness,
But hear me in my pain.
Accept distress, and support me with mercy.

People so often turn my glory to shame.
People love vanity and want lies,
And I often do their will.

I want to stand apart from falsity,
To respect myself.
I know that wonder and goodness are right.
At night, alone, my heart reflects love,
Offers sacrifice and trust.
But, afterwards, back in the world again,
Among companions, who can show me any good?

God, let your light penetrate my darkness.
Put gladness again into my heart.
Then, I may lay down in peace, and sleep in safety.

FIVE

You will hear my voice in the morning, chanting the power of good.
No pleasure lasts in wickedness;
Evil is without a permanent home.
Truth evaporates foolishness and helps iniquity betray itself.
The lying destroy their own meaning;
Life rejects violent and deceitful persons.

Creative energies, potent with gladness, full of mercy,
Help me to learn a life of careful distinctions.
Lesser goals dare not be my beacon.
Others cannot guide my path.
Let us all put our trust in goodness.
The power of good alone can defend us through all the tragic glories of life.

SIX

May the days be merciful, for I am weak.
Heal me, for my body is bent.
My soul is sore with the tribulations of life.
Save me!!
For death has no memory, and the grave is without praise.

Weary with groaning, nights awash in tears,
My spirit is consumed by grief,
Anxiety shortens my days.

Depart from me, iniquities!
In the Creator's presence, I am suddenly ashamed of my grief.

SEVEN

If I have been responsible for injustice, done evil to those at peace with me,
Made enemies without cause,
Then, let people persecute my soul and destroy my life,
Allow them to lay my honor in the dust,
To be angry with me and make their judgments.

Yet, may they also consider my actions for good,
My intentions of right, my attempts at justice.
May they also weigh my integrity,
And be merciful to the uprightness which still lives in my heart.

I know, Creator, that you must be angry with the wicked every day.
I believe that your spirit battles with injustice, mischief, lies.
Evil does come back, inexorably, upon its perpetrators.
They do fall into pits of their own making.
Let me be so trusting that I live to reflect your justice,
That I let your mercy enter my soul.

EIGHT

How excellent is all the universe in your name, Creation.
Awesome, starry cosmos, fecund, evolving Earth,
Strength rising in the words of children.
I am amazed at your orders. I wonder at your meanings.

My species are guardians of this planet,
With high visions, much glory and honor.
There is incredible power in our hands.
We have the responsibility of life or death for much of the living Earth.

Help us to magnify the light of the heavens,
To do justice to the energies of the Earth.
Give children love and patience to go with their strength.
Temper our power with your goodness.
How excellent is all the universe in your name, Creation.

Eagle Feather with children:
Vancouver, British Columbia, Canada

NINE

I shall praise life with my whole heart,
And point out all its marvelous works.
I shall be glad and rejoice.
I shall sing praise with real joy.

Evil perishes; ignorance is its own rebuke,
And the wicked destroy their souls.
May Creation serve as a refuge for the oppressed.
May the creative energies be a refuge for each of us,
In our times of trouble.

May we not forget the cries of humble people,
May we be merciful, and consider their troubles,
Lifting ourselves up from the gates of death,
While the ignorant sink down in the dark,
And malicious people get caught in their own schemes.
The needy will not always be deprived,
Nor will the poor live forever without wealth of their own.

There is a power beyond people,
And laws above any present structure.
We are children of a greater spirit.
Even the most powerful and wise are only children before God.

TEN

God waits – far away. Its will hidden in times of trouble.

Evil devises its imaginings recklessly.
Societies persecute their poor without effort.
The wicked often win, the covetous receive, the possessive gain wealth,
Cruel people glory in their strength.
Many discipline themselves against compassion and turn away from good.
People curse, practice deceit and fraud, live mischief and vanity,
And yet, adversity is not their portion.
They not only thrive; they corrupt and persecute:
Murdering innocence, stealing from the already disadvantaged,
Using their leisure to outwit the ignorant, their wealth to tax the poor.
These people believe in 'the survival of the fittest,'
And make no allowances for grace or goodness,
For compassion, sometimes, not even for love.

God waits – far away. Its will hidden in times of trouble.

Arise, powers of the universe, forget not the humble.
Help the orphan, bear the burdens of the poor,
Stand with us in the gales of our adversity.

May we be humane beings:
Living with love for our friends, and with compassion for all people,
Keeping faith in grace and goodness.
May we no longer oppress one another.

ELEVEN

I cannot flee, like a bird to the mountain;
For, I trust in the wisdom of acting rightly.
The vicious and mischief-makers will take advantage of morality and justice,
But if I do not uphold my principles,
What is the meaning of my life?

Life tries us all, and evil is often tempting.
But evil can be overcome, and we can turn away from violence.
In the wisdom of right actions, I face my god and behold my path.

TWELVE

Help! Goodness ceases.
Everyone flatters or boasts and speaks with double meanings.
Goodness does not need flattery nor pride.
What we are, what we shall be, are largely gifts from life and other people,
Even most of our words are not our own.
How can we, then, continue to oppress the poor and neglect the needy?

Goodness has the purity of countless tempered lives.
We may lose goodness, in our time, but it will be preserved,
Though the wicked walk everywhere and the vile be exalted in their brief days.
Goodness may be lost in our time, but it will be preserved.

THIRTEEN

God may forget me forever.
God's face will probably always remain hidden.
I must learn to take counsel in my own soul
Even when I have sorrows in my heart
And enemies for my neighbors.

I ask for the light of truth before I die.
May the truth cast out the shadows of my sorrow
And banish the hatred of my enemies.
If I can only see the truth
And sing the bountiful joys of existence, then I shall be saved,
And can live out my days with mercy and trust.

FOURTEEN

The fools say in their hearts, 'there is no God;
For, there is corruption, disease and abominable situations.
Everything seems to have an evil side.'
The fool's god looks down upon people, expecting perfection,
Pictures people who see a god without darkness
And reflect that god in all they do.
Such people do not exist.
Humans are covered with the dust, sweat, and the errors of life.
There is no perfect person, not one.

Nor is God without darkness
Except to those unmarked by failure and inner strife.
In their ignorance, fools disgrace humanity by rarifying God.
God is, indeed, right, justice, and goodness,
But God is also acceptance, evolution, and mercy.
How else could God counsel those in error, and be a refuge to all in their need?

We must learn to rise above our utopian dreams,
To accept the salvations of earthly life.
Our lives are a striving for goodness, a search for God,
In the captivity of error, and the awareness of neutrality, evil and darkness.
We must face the imperfections of ourselves and of our God
If our search is to lead us to rejoice and be glad.

FIFTEEN

Creator, who lives in your spirit?
It must be those who act with respect,
Who work with diligence for justice,
Who think truth, and say it.
Not the critic, the cruel, or the judge,
Not those busy condemning the weak,
But those who honor the loving,
Who speak their own truths and stand by them.
Not giving to receive back with interest,
Not seizing rewards by power,
But giving, as the essence of life.
Acclaiming the astounding rewards of fate.
Such spirit is eternal, and It moves the universe.

SIXTEEN

Preserve my god: for my soul is put in its trust.
I remain unsure; for though I believe in my god,
My soul seems frail and faint.
Others are excellent saints filled with ecstasy,
Yet my principles are also worthy.
Surely, it is those who pursue unworthy goals and fallen idols
Who shall suffer by their false steps and narrow visions?

My principles are my portion; my god is my foundation.
Life blesses me with a generous existence.
I want to live my beliefs, cherish my chosen goals, stand by my god;
For, my body exists in hope, and my spirit rejoices in its faith.
Preserve me from despair and corruption.
Show me the path of life.
I know its way is the fullness of joy,
That its spirit are the pleasures which endure.

SEVENTEEN

Hear the right.
My best intuitions are tried and true.
By human standards, I have not been destructive.
Keep me on a path of loving kindness.
Let me be as the pupil of a cosmic eye, the shadow of the horizon's wings.

Cruelty, malice, and carelessness do pervade the world,
But their practitioners get caught in indolence and pride,
Trapped by the fat in their own souls.
I know that I share in this waste and debilitation.
I, too, become greedy of prey for my selfish interests,
Am drawn to savor false mysteries, and to lurk in secret places.

Let us disappoint weakness and avarice, cast aside laziness and pride.
We remain God's hands on Earth.
Some are given glories, and others blessings,
But I shall be satisfied if I hear the right.
The right is the likeness of God on Earth.

EIGHTEEN

I shall love the source of my strength. I shall praise that which is worthy.
We are drawn from many waters, delivered from strong enemies.
Saved from most calamities.
Life surely delights in us.
We appear to be rewarded for righteousness,
To be recompensed for departing from evil.

The Creator is revealed in the merciful, in the upright person,
In the pure and the forthright.
Creation saves the afflicted, not by the fantastic or miraculous,
But by the humble acts of good people.
By supporting wisdom, Creation enlightens the darkness.
This energy for truth, justice, and goodness is the source of our strength.
It is worthy of our praise.

With this God, enemies are met with justice and conquered by love.
Its gentleness makes us great.
This God delivers us of ceaseless strivings, and gives our works meaning.
This God subdues our pride,
And lifts us above those who act with violence or vengeance.
In this God, there is no heathen or stranger, and mercy is its watchword.
I shall love the source of my strength, and praise that which is worthy.

Shoe Repair Man:
Bombay, India

NINETEEN

Glorious, starry heavens!
Universe radiating creative evolution.
Purposes appear evident; everything seems to demonstrate knowledge.
Connections and common energies reach throughout the Earth,
And into the boundaries of the cosmos.
To us, these seem a temple for the Sun.
This perpetual fire: our energy, our light,
Hypnotist of the world, like the eye of God.
The Sun is our center of the cosmic energies which make our lives possible.
It is the blazing symbol of universal spirit,
The words of power in Creation's mouth.

And the meditations of our hearts?
Our energies center in our faiths:
Personal perspectives on moral law, with its simple duties and wise conduct.
These seem to be the sermons of life.
The laws of humane conduct are straightforward,
Clear to those with the courage to open their eyes,
Cause for rejoicing among honest people, warnings for the weak,
Cleansing for those with the will to endure.

We cannot know the cosmic errors, nor stand in judgment of God's sins,
But we can keep ourselves from needless faults,
Refuse to oppress, and to presume upon, the lives of our neighbors.
Our words and the meditations of our hearts can make a just life possible.
Our words and the meditations of our hearts support our strength
And help to redeem the Spirit alive in the universe.

TWENTY

God, I need the amulet of your name.
Give me a sanctuary in the temple,
And a homeland secure in its strength.
Help me to make the necessary sacrifices,
To remember the gifts and wisdom of my own heart,
As it is anointed by your spirit.
I need your saving strength;
For, I do not trust the power of arms, nor the solutions of machines,
But simply the goodness of your laws, as I understand them.
Let me rise and stand upright and follow your call, in this, a time of trouble.

TWENTY-ONE

Your strength makes us each a ruler.
How many requests are answered?
Many humble people do gain their hearts' desires.
Goodness prevents much harm;
Our best works may be crowned with satisfaction.
We are given life, even a long life.
Honor and some majesty are often our portion.
Trust and mercy exist, and truth endures.
So, though there are reasons for fear,
Sincere people need not turn away from life.
They can praise its power and cherish its strength.

TWENTY-TWO

My God, my God, why have you forsaken me? You are far away and silent,
Although I cry aloud, and my country sings your praises.
My ancestors trusted, and you delivered them.
I feel like a worm, not a human being,
A reproach to my neighbors, despised by people.
They laugh at me, make light of my trials,
And shake their heads in disbelief, saying:
He thought God would deliver him; let him deliver himself out of his own pride.

You took me out of the womb and gave me hope at my mother's breasts.
Since my birth, you have been my God.
Be not far from me now; for trouble is near, and there is no one to help.
I am surrounded by destruction and anger,
And it turns my heart to wax, my fortitude to water.
My strength has dried up, and I am speechless, dust in the jaws of death.
Envious people surround me; many willingly wound me.
Staring at my weakness, they divide my garments; they seize my living.
Help me! Deliver me from their power.

I shall be faithful and praise your name.
For you have served the afflicted, you will hear my cry.
In time, all the Earth will know you and need you.
The body will die in the dust; none keep alive their own souls.
Only the seeds of faith will endure.
Deliver me from my pride.
Help me to live for those yet to be born.

TWENTY-THREE

By the grace of this world, we live.
We are fed by the green fields;
We drink and wash ourselves in its rushing waters.
When we stop to touch and be touched by nature,
Our spirits are restored.
Nature can help us understand the paths to virtue.
We shall die, and tragedy will befall us,
But the light we have discovered or reflected will live on.
One day of life, understood in its fullness, satisfies perfectly.
Practice goodness and mercy,
And open yourselves to these aspects of the world,
And your cup will overflow.

TWENTY-FOUR

The Earth in its fullness is the Creator's,
The whole world and all who dwell there.
The seas were established, and the ebb and flow of life.
Who can ascend to the stars,
Or can stand upright forever in the presence of nature's awesome powers?

Humans could live with cleaner hands and purer hearts,
Could lift their souls out of vanity and refuse to speak deceit.
The practice of truth is their salvation. It creates the seekers of God,
And these truthseekers experience the holy.

Open yourself to the truths of life:
Lift up your head, use your intellect,
Your will for good, your courage.
The grace of Earth, the glory of God, is open to you.
God will come to you, if you but look up to the peaks,
And take a stand beside the powers of grace.

Mountains Reflected:
Canadian Rockies

TWENTY-FIVE

I lift up my soul,
Do not let me be ashamed.
Help me to remember mercy and love; they endure,
Not the sins of youth, nor the bad habits of my days.
Rather keep me to mercy and to the instructive power of good.
For the meek do learn; many will, yet, be attentive to the law.
My mistakes are a multitude, my faults, glaring,
Forgive me my arrogance and error.

I am in awe of the world.
I can taste the danger of my own frailty before it,
And intuit power and purpose worthy of worship.
If we retain that awareness of danger, that awe of goodness,
Respect in our living those worthy purposes and powers,
We may dwell at ease, and our children will inherit the Earth.
This is the meaning of 'fearing God.'

Life is perilous, yet, we should and do attempt it.
This requires awareness, respect, love.
It asks for an awesome struggle for partnership
With the cosmos and the moral law.
These powers are worthy of fear,
Yet, they depend, in part, upon us for life in this world.
I lift my soul,
Do not let me be ashamed.

TWENTY-SIX

We must walk our own integrity.
We need to stand firm in the truths we perceive.
Experience and emotion will prove, or disprove, them;
Loving kindness will improve them.

We should choose our companions carefully,
Taking leisure with sincere people, and speech with honest thinkers.
No one lives in the midst of evil without being corrupted.
Neutrality is not innocent,
And we cannot wash our hands of the guilts of our time and land.
We must dare to speak up in protest, and in thanksgiving,
To praise wondrous works, and to honor the honorable.
We must refuse easy or pleasant community with bloody and treacherous elites,
Mischiefmakers, or those trying to purchase virtue with power.

We must walk our own integrity.
We need to be ready to accept such redemption and mercy as are freely given.
Let us stand on our chosen foundations.
Let us bless life.

TWENTY-SEVEN

My light and my salvation, what is to be gained by fear?
Truth is the strength of my life. Why should I be afraid of reality?
We have overcome tragedy and outlasted opposition,
Even built peace out of arguments and conflict.
My desire is to live in this world as Creation's temple,
To behold life's beauty all the days of my life, and ever to inquire after truth.

For the world has grace and beauty.
Let me answer its mercies with joy and peace.
Help me to seek the truth, face to face,
Even beyond the frontiers of my own traditions.
Life, teach me the way, lead me in a forthright path.
Deliver me from the practice or acceptance of falsity and cruelty.
Without goodness around me, I would have fainted away.
Let me be of good courage, and wait with patience for the truth.
The truth is nurtured by a steadfast heart.

Highland Heather:
Scotland

TWENTY-EIGHT

Be not silent.
Do not withdraw with the wicked,
Who speak peace to their neighbors,
But hold mischief in their hearts.
Give us each according to our deeds.
Let us receive the work of our own hands,
The saving grace of our individual endeavors.
Let the creative be built up,
And the destructive fade away.

TWENTY-NINE

Give yourselves, you mighty people.
Share your glory and your strength.
For these arise out of Creation's beauty and Creation's power,
Like mists rise off the sea.

The Creator's voice speaks through all being.
Its truth moves the tides of oceans, speaks in the silence of wilderness,
Lifts forests to the sky, and burns them,
Planting, again, seeds among the ashes.
The Creator gives birth to each new life,
Its truth is the eternal flame. Worship these creative powers.
Both the cosmos and the soul are its temples.
Its light dances in the eyes of children,
Shines equally from the dignified eyes of those about to die.

The Creator rides the flux of being.
It gives us strength, and will bless us.
Give yourselves, be Creation's people.

THIRTY

You have lifted us up.
Seeking truth, we were healed.
Drawn away from despair, we were re-dedicated to life,
Able to rise up singing.

Anger needs only last a moment,
While grace fills our days and our years.
We may weep during our dark nights,
But your spirit comes again with the light.
In prosperity, who can fail to believe?
You have given us courage and beliefs for troubled times.
When we are up against the wailing walls of life,
It is the spirit which preserves the body.

Dust cannot declare the truth.
The voices, energies, and wills of brave people are needed.
Creation, continue your helpful mercies.
Turn our grief into dancing,
Wrap us around with gladness.
May our joy help to amplify your grace.
Help us not to fail our impulses to courage and to love.
May we never again keep silent, when we feel an urge to praise.

THIRTY-ONE

I am like a broken vessel, yet let me never be ashamed.
For you are present, Creator, even in me,
And righteousness will endure.

My life seems to have been spent in grief, my years with sighing.
My strength has failed because of my iniquities.
I feel consumed in body and in soul.
My failures are painful even to my enemies, but tragic for my neighbors,
And fearful for my friends.
They flee at my appearance. They put me out of mind, as one would the dead.

I have heard the slanders of many.
How good it would be if those lying lips could be put to silence
Which speak grievous things so contemptuously against righteous people.
Righteousness comes not from perfection, but by sincere seeking after truth,
Not by pride, but by the humble acceptance of life's grace,
Not by power, but by faith.

You have set my feet, Creator, in a large room.
I easily become lost in my own life without the light of your truths.
Give me courage, and strengthen my heart with hope.

I am like a broken vessel, yet let me never be ashamed.
For you are present, Creator, even in me,
And righteousness will endure.

THIRTY-TWO

We are blessed for outgrowing our transgressions,
Forgiven, when we convert our sins into truthfulness and worthy actions.
We can honor those who do not mistake guile for their consciences,
Who discontinue their grave injustices.

Our mistakes speak louder than any creeds.
Our wickedness weighs heavier upon us than any other burden.
For, we are not mules who can be shut off from sin by bit and bridle,
Nor stones who can remain pure through inactivity.
We gain relief by admitting our errors and hypocrisies,
To those most affected, to ourselves, and to our God.

Trust grows out of learning from error,
But we cannot begin to learn without admitting the errors.
This is the beginning of forgiveness, and the heart of God's mercy.

THIRTY-THREE

Rejoice in Creation.
Praise is the essence of righteous people.
Use all of your skills, and live honestly.
Admit your awe of the universe, and your fears about life.

All human hearts have been fashioned alike
And depend upon one another for their sustenance.
We are not delivered by our strength, but by acting with hope.
We are not saved by our own powers, but by the practice of cooperation.
Live by hope and mercy.

THIRTY-FOUR

Our souls shall make their boasts in Creation.
The humble will hear another praised and be glad.
This praise magnifies the God within, so it exalts us all.
Praising the Creation can deliver everyone from their fears.

Look at the light, and the shadows pass away.
Taste and see that Creation is good.
Blessed are those able to trust.
Depart from habits of wrong,
But, further, do good, and love your many days.
Seek paths to peace and walk them patiently.

Our part in Creation is knowledge, and support for goodness;
It is strength and forgiveness in overcoming evil;
It is passion, tempered by facing imperfections, saved by humbled spirits.
Our souls shall make their boasts in Creation.

THIRTY-FIVE

Though you simply look on in silence,
I shall give thanks to you in the great congregation
And praise you among the people.

I want to wash away hate and to quiet deceit,
To help the mentors of evil to be ashamed and brought into confusion,
To assist foolish pride in being dishonored, and goodness to be magnified.

Though you simply look on in silence,
I wish to have sympathy even when the wicked are sick,
And to focus my corrective powers upon disciplining and strengthening myself.

May I join with friend and sibling to mourn the pain of the Earth.
Though adversaries rejoice and join in my unceasing torment,
Mock my feasts and secretly speak against me, I shall speak of your truth
And praise you all the day long,
Though you simply look on in silence.

Stave Church:
Norway

THIRTY-SIX

You are the fountain of life, but, because of our transgressions, we fear you.
We flatter ourselves, yet our iniquities make us hateful in our own eyes,
We could be wise and do good;
Instead, we devise mischief in our beds and bad manners at our tables.
Your mercy fills the skies, yet, we do not abhor evil.
Where ever we look deeply, there is clarity and judgment.
High in the mountains, deep in the seas, you preserve life.

Our love grows out of the trust we have in life.
From the kindness of your days, we are surrounded by the joys of existence
And splash in the rivers of your pleasures.
In your light, we see the light.

Let not pride come between us and the essence of life,
Nor wickedness remove us from the paths of its abundance.
Help us to practice loving-kindness and to be upright in heart.
You are the fountain of life.
Help us to correct our errors and to discipline our desires,
While discovering that we do not need to live in fear

THIRTY-SEVEN

The meek shall inherit the Earth, while wickedness withers like the weeds.
Be not obsessed by evil,
Neither worry yourself with the prosperity of wickedness.
Trust in the truth, and do good.
You will survive and, even, flourish.
Delight yourself with life; commit yourself to worthy principles.
Your integrity will find the light; your good judgments will sparkle.

Rest in the creation and wait patiently for the harvest of goodness.
Do not worry about the success of others, or the prosperity of wickedness.
Cease from anger and forsake wrath.
Do not worry yourself into evil ways.

Wickedness withers away, while the patient and the meek
Reap the great inheritance, the abundance of peace.
Drawing out their swords, evil people end by rending their own hearts.
Their weapons will be broken; their plots will fail.
The little that a good person has is better than the riches of many wicked;
For, good people do not need to be ashamed
And can still satisfy themselves in bad times,
While evil-doers perish even in their wealth,
And are consumed by the burdens of their ways.
The wicked borrow from life, and do not repay,
While good people give freely, and live each day with mercy
And receive these in return.

Delight in the paths of love, let Creation be in your heart.
Notice the truthful person and behold upright acts,
For the end of these paths is peace.

THIRTY-EIGHT

Creator, there seems to be no soundness in the midst of the world's anger;
Neither do I have any rest from my failures and weakness.
The burden of my sins is too heavy for me to bear.
My heart pants, my strength fails,
And the light of my eyes has gone out.
My intimates and my friends stand aloof; my kin are far away.
My opponents seem lively and strong.
Many people appear to render evil for good.
Forsake me not, Creator,
Nor rebuke me further in life.

THIRTY-NINE

I took heed of my ways, and kept silent for a time,
Allowing good to be unprotected by my voice.
It stirred my sorrow and made my soul burn:
Truth, unprotected by my prophesies, light uncherished by my words.

Yet, it showed me my own frailty.
How small is my part; how quickly passing is my time.
We do seem vain in the face of the universe,
Insignificant in relation to the eternal truths.

However, our hope is a part of that eternal,
An active atom in that universe.
In that light, I shall dare, again,
To speak my truth and to live out my faith.

Tea Ceremony:
Japan

FORTY

The Creator has put a new song into my mouth with trust in its power:
Respect not the proud, turn aside from lies,
Bring yourselves up out of the clay pits onto a rock,
Wait patiently for the Creator.
Its wonderful works beyond enumeration.
It does not desire offerings for sins.

The Creator's law is within our hearts.
Reveal faithfulness, loving-kindness, truth and tender mercies.
Believe in the goodness of the human heart, and in the grace of life.
Reveal and believe in these virtues even when your iniquities take hold of you.
Though your sins be many, look up into the light of the Creator.
Think of the poor and the needy, and do your part to help with Creation.
Rejoice and be glad in the Creation's life.

FORTY-ONE

Blessed are those who are considerate of the poor.
They will receive mercy in their own times of trouble.
Their lives will medicate and bring solace to many souls.
Their own works save them, even from the wills of their enemies.
Although their best friends turn away, or many devise their hurt,
Disease and weakness plague them,
Yet, they will be upheld by their own integrity.

FORTY-TWO

Where is my God?
As a thirsty animal rushes after water so do I seek you.
I thirst after the living God.
With joy and praise, with the multitude and during holidays,
By pouring out my soul in hope and tears,
I seek your countenance, desire your trust.

Why is my soul downcast?
Why have I allowed myself to be so disquieted?
Deep calls onto deep.
The waves of the seas of creation wash over the tears of my faith.

Where is my God?
The loving-kindness of the days,
The songs of the night, and the prayers of my life,
The pain of my enemies' reproaches, the disquiet and humility of my soul,
And the health of my countenance,
These must be my God, the living God of my life.

FORTY-THREE

Judge me, Creator, and plead my cause against an ungodly nation.
Deliver me from participation in lies and injustice.
Help me to overcome the oppressions in my nation.
Spread your light and your truth.
Let the health in my spirit overcome the anxieties within me.
Let my heart be an altar for Creation.

FORTY-FOUR

Our parents have told us of God's work in ancient times.
Your power gave us this land and made us a people.
It was not the strength of our fathers' weapons,
But the light of your countenance that made us a nation.
It was not the pride of our mothers' works,
But the truth of your principles that gave us a home.
You are our Creator.
Save us from the slyness of Jacob.
I shall not trust in my sword nor my pride, but in you.

Arise! Redeem us with your mercy.
We feel cast off and put to shame.
Our enemies turn us away, and we are a scattered people.
When we are worth nothing, it does not increase your wealth.
We do not want to be a reproach, nor a source of derision.
Our name, now, is a byword for tragedy.
We cause our neighbors to shake their heads at a life of faith.

Yet, our hearts are still with you.
We continue our pledges to walk in your way.
Awake! Do not cast us aside, nor hide your face from our afflictions.
Arise! Redeem us with your mercy.

FORTY-FIVE

Each of us is, in our heart, a glorious ruler,
A graceful child of God with our own glory and majesty.
Power is in our hands.
If we will do good and forsake evil,
Gladness will be in our hearts.

Our energies create their own perfumes.
Others will recognize our grace,
And may join in the special adventures of our lives.
Strangers will praise us, giving us paths to our own powers.
Our parents' strengths, and our own abilities,
Will make our children rulers with the Earth.
A life of virtue is the best praise of God.

Vigeland Statues:
Oslo, Norway

FORTY-SIX

Creation is a very present help.
Though mountains fall into the seas, or seas explode,
Even when Earth itself begins to disappear,
Creation remains a great and peaceful stream.
Creation flows from the beginning of time,
Through us, into eternity.

Life and the world are full of desolations.
But even wars cease, and forests grow upon the ashes.
Be still, and understand Creation.
Believe in your refuge and your strength.
Flow with the eternal stream.

FORTY-SEVEN

Clap your hands, all you people.
Shout to God with voices of triumph.
The Creator is all the energies of the Earth.
Life subdues every person; no nation is eternal,
And our inheritances are chosen for us.
Yet, we are ruled by a spirit.
God goes up with a shout, out among us in music.

Sing praises, sing praises with understanding.
All powers are gathered together.
Energies should have purpose,
And we should know enough to live by praise, and to praise by living.
Honest celebration is the way of the spirit.

FORTY-EIGHT

The city of God is a woman in childbirth,
A mountain of life, the joy of the whole Earth.
This is the living beauty of holiness, the real symbol of refuge.
Men marvel, are troubled, and hasten away.
Fear takes hold, for there is pain in labor, agony in creativity.
Tragedy is the actual shadow on the edge of new life.

We love God, but living god in rightness and loving kindness,
This is the travail of a woman in labor,
The gladness of a mother at her child's birth.
Mighty is the city of God,
A mountain of life, our guide, even unto death.

FORTY-NINE

Hear this, inhabitants of the world:
Low and high, rich and poor, together:
Our iniquities come back to surround us;
They are the sources of our fears.
Those who trust in possessions, or who live by pride
Can by no means redeem their comrades,
Or even provide a ransom for themselves.

Redemption can only be done by the living.
The soul is the precious gift of life.
Once dead through disuse and corruption, it ceases forever.
We know that even the wisest seers died.
Each person perishes, leaving her wealth to others.
It is not our pride which endures, but our goodness,
The light we have dared to share.
Imagined acts disappear,
Even the strongest house crumbles,
But Creation redeems our souls from the powers of the grave.
For our souls are Its children;
They are our portions of the eternal light.

We carry no wealth or arrogance away to the grave,
Yet, the essential is not lost in death.
Realize the light in yourself! Do well by life, and your soul will endure.
While those who honor their possessions, or who live by their pride,
May even lose their souls during life.
Ceasing to see the light, they perish like beasts.

FIFTY

Creation calls the rising and the setting sun.
Its light is a perfection of beauty.
This light does not remain abstract.
It burns in the fires of the Earth,
In the hearths and hearts of living men and women.
The heavens shine, goodness streams from vibrant eyes,
Warmth radiates from the hands and principles of people.

Why offer Creation burnt flesh and streaming blood?
Arrogant violence is surely misplaced sacrifice.
Offer Creation, thanksgiving. Fulfill your vows of goodness,
And call upon the Creator's help in the midst of real trouble.
These acts glorify Creation, and deliver you.

Wicked people may make laws and mouth covenants,
But they hate instruction, and cast their words behind them.
They consent with thieves, partake with adulterers,
Speak evil of others, lie, even work against their own siblings.
Yet, beauty, truth, and goodness endure.
Not only in the light of Creation,
But deep in the fires of our hearts.
All of us have been wicked,
Yet every one of us is capable of praise,
Is potent with possibilities of light.
This is the salvation of life.

FIFTY-ONE

Loving-kindness is the meaning of mercy.
The multitude of Creation's mercies blot out human transgressions,
Washing away iniquity, cleansing us of sins.
Yet, I must acknowledge that evil remains alive in my heart.
Perhaps we are conceived in sin, or shaped by corrupt cultures,
Though truth is desired within, and the heart does flourish in wisdom.
By causing us to hear joy and gladness, Creation breaks the bones of evil,
And makes us, again, whiter than snow.
From blood-guiltiness, we are saved to sing aloud.
Our lips are open, our mouths are full of praise

The real sacrifices to Creation are the disciplines of the spirit:
Not broken bones, but tempered pride,
Not burnt offerings, but the light of truth,
Not proud dogmas, but a contrite faith,
Not despising, but delight.
Doing good with pleasure,
Such disciplines are the sacrifices of righteousness,
The living offerings for Creation's altar.

FIFTY-TWO

Why do humans boast in the face of God?
Our tongues are Jacob's razors, working deceit, loving evil more than good,
Devouring with our deeds.

Human finitude is there for all to see.
It makes our mightiness laughable.
We fail to make Creation our strength.
We trust rather in our riches, and strengthen ourselves in wickedness.

May we choose a different path:
Be like a tree standing tall in the trust of God for years on end.
This is a path of genuine might, and a life worthy of praise.

FIFTY-THREE

The fools have said in their hearts:
'There is no God; the world is full of corruption,
And no one is consistently good.
We are all lost in the confusion and darkness of life.'
We are in great fear, where there needs be no fear.
Everyone has retreated from their quests, given up their trust in life.

Creation looks for the seekers:
Those who live to understand, who dare to do good,
Who have the courage to call upon God when they are devoured,
As they praise God when they have bread to eat.

The seekers will overcome even the concept 'enemy,'
Will outlive the need to be ashamed, will go beyond the desire to despise.
Salvation is captive in no land, bound to no city.
All that try shall rejoice, and every person can be glad.

FIFTY-FOUR

God is not saved, nor saves, by being named.
We cannot define divine strength,
Nor is judgment God's transparent way.

Strangers may rise up against us, if we forget them.
Oppressors may seek after our souls, if we judge them.
If we forswear and condemn, we can expect evil rewards,
And shall live to see our truths cut off.

Praising God requires a different kind of sacrifice.
God delivers out of trouble by helping us to remember the stranger,
And by showing us ways to nurture the worthiness in our enemies.

FIFTY-FIVE

Oh, that I had wings like a dove; then, I would fly away and be at rest.
Hasten my escape from the windy storms and tempests of life.
I would wander far off.

For the city of life is filled with violence and strife.
Guile surrounds my days.
Even my friends and guides, those sweet people with whom I took counsel,
Have war in their hearts, their words are drawn swords.
Even these friends reproach me and magnify themselves against me.
I could have borne the reproach of enemies and strangers,
But how can I hide myself from my guides, protect myself from my friends?

These friends have broken our covenant.
They do not support me in my need, nor accept me in my weakness.
I cry aloud, and they refuse to hear.
Is it because they have no present crisis, that they are without fear?
Do they not suffer and, yet, remain unmoved?

I am suffering:
Mourning in my weakness, divided in my soul,
Abandoned by my friends.
I want to cast my burden on the Creator,
And hope that God will hear, and gives me rest.

Oh, that I had wings like a dove; then, I would fly away and be at rest
Hasten my escape from the windy storms and tempests of life.
I would wander far off.

FIFTY-SIX

When I am afraid, Creation can be my defender.
Praise and trust draws out the fear caught in my flesh.
I trust in Creation, while people seem to swallow me up.
Their attentions oppress me.
They bend words, gather themselves in enmity,
Hide themselves from intimacy, criticize, and expect failures.

As people swallow me up, may Creation swallow my fears.
The book of life contains those fears, but it is not ruled by them.
Help me to turn my fears back, to remember that Creation is in me.
Living the eternal truths, I need not be afraid.

FIFTY-SEVEN

My soul is among lions, and I live with people set on fire.
Their deeds are slings and arrows of outrageous fortune;
Their tongues are well-sharpened swords.
Only the shadow of your mercy can save me from these calamities.
I shall awake early in your praise and trust you in the dead of night.
My heart is fixed, Creator, my heart is fixed.
I shall sing praise to you, exalted Creation,
Whose mercy performs all wonders, whose truth surrounds the Earth.

Lion with Kill:
Tanzania, East Africa

FIFTY-EIGHT

Congregations are fat with righteousness.
People are propped upon their condemnations of others.
How well we like to judge:
Spewing our anger out in acid streams upon the bodies of the struggling world.
Infants speak no lies,
Nor are children estranged completely, yet, from the grace of life.
We must be given time to learn distrust,
To practice anger until it freezes into hate.
We must have time to lose the charms of life,
As young lions break their teeth by gnawing bones,
To melt away in the rushing waters of the world,
As arrows to be lost in grass.

Hardening ourselves with righteous, vengeance, harsh judgments,
We become barnacles.
Each birth is untimely; no one sees the Sun.
If we recognized that whirlwinds gather only dust,
That being angry is not being true;
Then, we could rejoice and not need vengeance,
Nor the blood of others to save our own meaning.
In judging the Earth, God meditates upon Its own being.

FIFTY-NINE

Deliver me from the heathen, Creator.
Your mercy touches all races, nations and faiths.
Heathen howl in every city, run loose across all the fields of the Earth.
The heathen are given godly souls, yet, they choose to act like beasts,
In fact; worse than beasts. They plan wickedness; they punish without fault.
They make swords of their lips, and sins of their days.

Slay them not, lest we forget,
But scatter them, so that we are not consumed.
Let them return, howling like the dogs in search of meat.
We can understand them.
It is always easy to become heathen.

Let no one remain a human beast, intent, simply, on meat or howling.
Let us all, instead, find the power to sing, to sing aloud of mercy in the morning.

SIXTY

Creator, you have shown us tragedy.
You have made us drink the wine of astonishment.
Why, now, have you cast us off, and scattered us?
Turn yourself to us again.
You, who have made the earth tremble and have broken it in great cracks,
Heal its awesome wounds.

Give banners again to those who live in reverence and truth,
Whose motive is your service.
Join the faithful from all tribes and sects of the Earth.
Give us help from trouble.
We dare not return alone, but with you, we could do valiantly.

SIXTY-ONE

Hear my cry, Creator; attend to my prayer.
Though it be from the end of the Earth, and when my heart is overwhelmed,
Still, lead me to the rock that is higher than me.

You have been my shelter, my strong tower,
And I shall trust in the shadows of your love forever.
Yet, hear my vow: lead me to the rock that is higher than me.

Allow me the heritage of the faithful. Prolong the generations of the good,
Succor mercy and truth, give me the power of praise,
That I may perform each day my vow: Lead me to the rock that is higher than me.

SIXTY-TWO

God has spoken once, twice, many times have I heard:
Power belongs to the Creator.
Leaning on other people is like depending upon tottering fences.
People, so often, have blessings in their mouths, but curses in their souls.
Mischief clothes them; lies are their ready defense.
God seems the only true protection.
We pour out our hearts to the Creator.
This is our refuge; this is our peace.

People in depression and failure do not do justice to life,
While those caught in pride and success forget about its tragic realities.
Trust neither human vanity, nor despair.
Do not become proud with borrowed riches, nor fond of historic sorrows.
Steel yourself against the traps of your own successes,
And against the swamps of your particular failures.
Power belongs to God, and mercy is also the Creator's.
Creation gives to each according to our daily acts,
And our willingness to embrace the future, to love the world beyond our self.

SIXTY-THREE

Creator, my soul thirsts after you. My flesh longs for you
In a dry and thirsty land where there is no water for the soul.

I have felt you in the sanctuary, but I crave the sight of you in the streets.
Your eternity may be better than life, but I am living.
Let me see your power and glory.
Satisfy my soul with your presence, fill my mouth with the joy of your being.

I remember you in my intimacy, and I meditate on you in the night watches
Because you have been my help.
In the shadow of your power, I would rejoice.
My soul follows hard at your heels, your right hand upholds me.
Satisfy my cravings for union with thee.

SIXTY-FOUR

Preserve my life, not from fear, nor from seeing evil,
But rather from doing evil out of fear.
Hide my cravings from the secret counsels of the wicked.
Hide my failures from the insurrections of anarchists and nihilists.
Critics and bitter people abound.
They continue to mutter in secret at those with the courage to act,
Against those whose integrity holds the world together.
They carp and criticize with little fear of grave consequences.

The doers of good have no time for whining.
While those who support evil, by what they do or leave undone,
Can gossip among themselves, support their joint weaknesses,
And avoid setting standards by accepting current trends.
By discovering the cravings and failures of others,
They justify their own evil deeds and sick dreams.

Preserve my life, not from fear, nor from seeing evil,
But rather from doing evil out of fear.
Everyone should fear straying from truth.
People who are afraid to do injustice, afraid to live without love.
They are a saving remnant who can trust in themselves,
And in all honest people, who can glory in the Creation.

SIXTY-FIVE

We may, yet, fulfill the promise of life,
Purge away our transgressions, and be satisfied with the Earth's goodness.
God answers our questions with reality, confronts our aggressions with power,
Stills the tumult of the peoples with the stillness of being.
Each of us is chosen to aid in creation.
None of us should miss rejoicing at morning and evening.
No one is oblivious to awe.

How rich and fertile are the Earth.
How beautiful is the river of your people.
How full and lively are the oceans of life, the universe of being.
Steep hills flower, and deserts bloom.
Pastures grow in wilderness; harvest returns.
The little hills rejoice on every side.
The pastures are clothed with flocks, the valleys with grain.
They, we, all being, shout for joy, and also sing.

Aerial View:
Malaysian Peninsula

SIXTY-SIX

Make a joyful noise all ye lands. Sing forth the honor of creation.
Life has terrible powers,
And uses them in ways which put fear in every person's heart.
Worship is not done without awe. We are not equals with God.
Our dialogue with the divine is caught in the inexorable grip
Of universal powers and eternal forces beyond our wildest dreams.
Rebellious people need not exalt themselves. God's will is done.

Creation holds our souls in life, controls the energies of our spirits.
By the tragedies and trials of life, Creation proves us,
Tempers us, like a precious metal.
Creation brings us into life and afflicts us.
Creation connects us with other people, and they use us.
Creation tries us by a river of failures and through a mountain of frustrations,
And brings each of us to our own golden harvests.

I shall use my energies in the service of Creation.
I shall keep the promises I have made when I was in trouble,
Even when I am fat and happy.

SIXTY-SEVEN

God is mercy, and it blesses us.
Its love shines warm upon us. God's way can be known here on Earth.
Its saving health lives among all nations.
Joy, praise of life, awe and wonder; these, God needs from us.
Justice can be done! Order does grow among the living of the Earth.
People, let's praise, using our energies for joy;
Then, shall the Earth yield its harvests, and God within shall bless us.

SIXTY-EIGHT

As smoke drifts away, so does hate dissipate.
As wax melts in the fire, so does wickedness disappear in the face of Creation.
Each of us can do good, can be glad, and rejoice in the light of Creation.

Let us be mothers to the motherless, a spouse to the widow,
Creation puts the solitary ones into families, and frees the oppressed.
Cynics may dwell forever in a dry land,
But Creation marched through the wilderness of Sinai,
Rain came to the desert when we were weary,
And there was goodness for the poor.
We rose from among the cooking pots on the silver wings of doves,
Touched by the gold of the Sun, we leaped up like a high hill,
A mighty band of holiness, full of gifts.
Even the rebellious lost their cynicism in the blinding brightness of the light.

Kingdoms of the Earth, rebuke the company of spears,
Scatter the people that delight in war.
Ascribe your power to Creation.
The Creator may be far off in the clouds,
Yet, the Creation, ultimately, gives power to the people of peace.

SIXTY-NINE

I sink into the swamp of my own feelings.
Passions flood my soul; life's deeps are swallowing me up;
Reproach has broken my heart. I am too weary to cry,
And my eyes fail while I wait for you, God.
Reproaches meant for you are ringing in my ears.
Whatever I do becomes a bad example to my people,
A song for drunkards to sing.
Let not passions' floods wash me away,
Neither let life's deeps swallow me up.

I looked for some to take pity, but there were none,
And for comforters, but I found no one.
That which should have been for my welfare has become a trap.
You know my foolishness, have seen all the reproaches,
Felt the shame, lived every dishonor.
My adversaries are all before you.
Why do you allow those who have been given little,
Who already suffered much, to be further oppressed, to suffer also tomorrow?
Why add to the grief of those already so wounded by life?

Let the passions return to their currents.
Help life's deeps to reflect peace and light.
Allow reproach to temper and inspire courageous hearts.
Let my faith and my days be not songs for drunkards in despair,
But songs of faith in life.

Freedom Statue:
Uganda, East Africa

SEVENTY

Make haste, Creator, to deliver me;
For I am poor, needy, and cannot wait much longer.
Do not confound me with intricacies of life or scripture.
My soul cannot survive if it remains so ashamed of its ignorance.
Quiet those around me savoring their criticisms.
Let us all seek to rejoice and be glad in the Creation.
In praise, we are all magnified.
Make haste, Creator, to deliver me;
For I am poor, needy, and cannot wait much longer.

SEVENTY-ONE

I have put my trust in you since my youth.
Now, when I am old, do not forsake me, never let my soul grow confused.
You have always been my rock, my strong habitation.
Your commandments have been there, in crisis, to save me.
You are ever my hope, have kept me upright throughout my many days.
I may be the wonder of some, but you are my refuge,
And my praise shall be continually of you.

Forsake me not, now, when my strength fails.
Some say that the old are forsaken, confound and reproach them.
I shall hope continuously, and praise you more and more.
How could I do less?
I perceive no limits to your love, no end to your gigantic works.

Life is tragic, filled with troubles and hurts.
Growing old is a painful drama,
Potent with disappointment in others and oneself.
My days are mostly past.
Still, I ask you to renew me, once again,
To quicken my spirit this time even more.
Bring me up, again, from the depths of the earth, in the twilight days of my life.
It will increase your greatness, by allowing me to radiate your spirit,
Increase your order, by tolerating my comfort.

I want to show your strength also to this generation.
I want to sing your Psalms once more,
Rejoice again in these twangings of the harp.
But, even more, I want to reflect the harmony of my soul,
Redeemed, once again, by you.

SEVENTY-TWO

Creator, share your wisdom with the rulers.
Help the leaders practice your justice among us.
They judge us all with their deeds.
They bring war or peace to the hills, poverty or plenty to the common people.

Creator, destroy every oppressor, and save the children of the poor.
Let the powerful continually fear your wrath,
And the weak always be able to trust in your grace.
You come down like rain upon the mown grass, like showers watering the earth.
You do justice and renew our souls.
Your dominion reaches from the depths of the sea to the heart of the Sun.
Those who dwell in wilderness still know you.
Everyone walks in your shadow.
All people offer their gifts.
Every nation serves you.

Redeem our souls from deceit and violence.
Help us to keep you living by treating all people and life as precious.
This reverence for life is the heart of prayer and the essence of praise.
A handful of leaders living by this code of precious life
Could make the cities flourish like the grass,
Would bless each being with Creation's wondrous grace.

Powerful leaders, let the whole Earth be filled with Creation's glory.
This will fulfill the prayers of all people.

SEVENTY-THREE

How easy it is to envy the wicked. So often, they do prosper.
They seem untroubled, unplagued by common concerns, fearless of death.
Some possess almost more than could be wished for.
Many increase their riches and prosper in the world,
Yet, a full cup of life will be wrung from them.

The pride of the wicked binds them like a chain.
Violence weighs upon them like a heavy coat.
Their vision is hidden in fatness; corruption makes them all oppressors.
The ungodly may reject God, slander their neighbors,
Heap ridicule upon life.
Yet, a full cup of life will be wrung from them.

Caught in this envy of the prosperity of the wicked,
I have felt that cleanliness of heart was in vain,
That chosen innocence was a waste.
I have been plagued and chastened by life.
I was afraid of offending future generations,
Pained by my own errors, and by the injustices of life.
However, I finally returned to the sanctuary of your law,
And understood that my envy was false.

The wicked are set in slippery places,
And they slide down to destruction.
In a moment, they are consumed by terrors.
They awake, as from a dream, without honor or resources,
Despising themselves.
How foolish it is to envy the wicked,
Who remain beasts without cleanliness of heart.
Flesh and heart fail without the guidance of the law.
Cleanliness of heart is close to the image of Creation.
A full cup of life will be wrung from us all.

SEVENTY-FOUR

Creator, why have you cast us off?
Remember this congregation. We are part of your inheritance.
See our desolation. Noise disrupts the peace.
War destroys and defiles what past generations have built up.
We are without prophets, bereft of leadership.
Shall people blaspheme your name forever?

It is your honor to work salvation in the midst of life.
Dividing the seas, giving sustenance to people in the wilderness.
In your arms, waters rise from the deserts, and great floods abate.
In your eyes, the seasons pass.

We are your doves among a multitude of wicked.
Forget not the congregation of the poor among the blasphemies of the foolish.
Caught in this dark world of cruelty are the keepers of your law.
Let not the oppressed remain ashamed.
In helping them, you plead your own cause.
Quiet the rising tumult of the foolish with the radiant light of your sun.

SEVENTY-FIVE

That you are near, your wondrous works declare.
As we receive our neighbors, it is our opportunity to do justice.
This is our responsibility as human beings:
To use our reason, to practice goodness,
To have more mercy than prideful righteousness.
Grace arises not from pride, or even skill, but from creation.
You pour a cup of life for each of us,
And each is given the chance to drink it with joy,
Or, to lose ourselves in the dregs, and be thrown out to fertilize the fields.
It is our choice and your power for us to be destroyed or exalted.

Girl with Mirror:
Bali, Indonesia

SEVENTY-SIX .

Please restrain humanity's wrath.
Break the weapons of war; store away the shields of defense.
For, the stout-hearted are spoiled:
Sleeping through their loves, too exhausted with anxiety to care.

Cast the rushing engines of fear and war into peaceful disuse.
Make people afraid enough of themselves to be still and calm.
Save each one of the meek of the earth.
Transform the energies of wrath into praise, joy, and love.
In this spirit, people will repay life's grace.
May it become terrible to be a wrath-maker in the earth.

SEVENTY-SEVEN

I remembered God, and was troubled.
I complained, and my spirit was overwhelmed.
My soul refused to be comforted.
All the wounds of my life reopened, and I wondered where mercy could be.

God, I have considered the days of old, the years of ancient times.
I have communed with my own heart,
And have made a diligent search of human knowledge.
Yet, I am so troubled that I can scarcely speak.
Will you cast me off forever?
Have you forgotten to be gracious?
Has anger shut you up?

Perhaps all this is my own infirmities.
I shall try again to remember the works of creation, the wonders of old.
You are the God which goes wonders. Your strength has redeemed the people.
Your deeds pour forth like mighty oceans.
The waters reflect your works, but their deeps are troubled by your passing,
Your footsteps are not known.

You lead us like a storm:
The earth trembles, the clouds pour, voices rumble in the night,
And the flashes of your light disturb and confound your human flock.

Clouds:
Indonesia

SEVENTY-EIGHT

Let us utter again dark sayings of old, what we have heard and known.
What our parents have told us.
We shall not hide our parable or its laws from our children,
Nor hide it from the generations to come.
We shall praise God and tell them of the wonders of creation,
And of our way with the Creator.

May we not be as our ancestors have been:
Stubborn and rebellious generations
Whose spirit was not steadfast in creation,
Who refused to walk in the Creator's law.

In the land of Egypt, God turned the rivers to blood,
And sent terrible plagues upon the oppressors.
Their first–born died,
And Israel went forth like sheep to pasture in the wilderness.
The Creator divided the sea, standing the waters up in walls,
Whirled like a pillar of cloud in the days, a column of fire in the nights.
Creation drew waters from the rocks, manna from the skies,
And doubt and lust from his people.

God's anger was kindled. He slew the worst of the people;
Others, he consumed in their vanity, their years were filled with trouble.
The people flattered God, but their words were lies.
Their deeds were not steadfast, their hearts full of guile.
Nevertheless, being full of compassion,
Again and again, the Creator turned his angel away.
He remembered that they were but flesh,
That they were a wind that passes and does not come again.

Generation after generation, we have tempted and provoked God,
And Creation has withheld its wrath.
We have bloated ourselves with pride, and worshipped idols.
And our pride has been struck down, our idols broken,
Our weapons made worthless, our homes divided.
Yet, we have been protected in your sanctuaries.
Creation still feeds those with integrity of heart,
And guides each of us, as we use the skills of our days.

SEVENTY-NINE

The temple of your people has been defiled.
Its stones are scattered. Your saints are consumed by vultures.
Jerusalem is washed in blood.
We have become a reproach to our neighbors,
A source of scorn and derision for those who do not care for us.

God, why are you always angry at your erring servants?
Yet, not angry at those who do not even know your name,
Who trod the temple of your people in the dust?
Why whip us again for past iniquities,
When carnage is fresh piled to the skies by those who scorn your name?
By the greatness of your power, preserve us who seem appointed to die.

EIGHTY

Turn to us again, Creator, cause your face to shine, and we shall be saved.
For so long you have been angry against the prayers of your people.
Giving them only tears for food and drink, making of us little but foolish strife.

Yet, it was you who brought this vine out of Egypt,
Who planted it in this soil, and let it take deep root.
Once, it covered this land with its shadow.
Now, all pluck of its fruits, and trod its shade to the ground.

Creator, visit this vine; for it is consumed in fires of strife,
And it perishes by your absence.
Once, you made it strong for yourself.
Turn to us again, Creator, cause your face to shine, and we shall be saved.

EIGHTY-ONE

Sing aloud to Creation!
Take a psalm, cymbals, and a harp.
Blow the trumpet and celebrate the feasts.

At the beginning, we did not know your language.
Since shouldering our burdens, and being delivered from years of servitude,
We stand well tested now by life and history.
It is our intention to worship no strange god, yet we get lost in our hearts' lusts,
Caught in our own foolish counsels.
Feed us with the honey bread of your being,
And we shall reflect your strength forever.

EIGHTY-TWO

God judges among the gods.
The Creator leads the congregation of the mighty.
Why does Creation accept wicked persons?

Creation should do justice to the afflicted, the needy, the poor, and the orphans.
Instead, it seems that the foundations of the Earth are out of course.
For the wicked survive.
They know not, neither will they understand.
They walk on in darkness.

Our God has said, to all people: you are gods, children of my spirit.
But you will die, like all flesh, and will stumble in your pride.
We shall await your justice, Creator, for all people are your inheritance.

Mosque Interior:
Israel

EIGHTY-THREE

At the heart of my faith, and the faith of my enemies, is this grave flaw:
They would destroy me, and cut my people off from being a nation,
And I would have them dead, and condemn their claims as a people.

Thus, even the worst enemies confederate with their foes.
We all make ourselves the dung of the Earth.
Who said that anyone could take possession of the dwellings of God?
What place is not God's dwelling?

Let all this pride be confounded.
All this righteous vengeance and violent hate be put to shame.
Help us to share your peace, Creator. To live as children of your universal law.

EIGHTY-FOUR

Every sparrow finds a place. No bird is without a nest for her young.
Let me dwell with you in the house of creation.

Life has its green valleys and its rushing streams.
People build their sanctuaries of peace, their temples of dream,
Where they can draw waters from the depths of their souls.

Blessed are those who see God in their fields and neighbors,
Who praise God in the streets. They go from strength to strength.
For them, God appears in everyone.
God is both sun and shade,
Gives both grace and glory.

No good thing will be withheld from those that trust in life.
How amiable is the world for those that love the world
As God's holy temple.

EIGHTY-FIVE

Mercy and truth are met together.
Righteousness and peace are found in a single embrace.
Truth springs out of the earth. Mercy grows upon forgiveness and love.
We cannot sustain nature, nor practice mercy,
Nor expect the truth to survive without the constant practice of love.
Righteousness does not ripen into meaning,
Unless all anger is shed, all pride discarded.
Peace finds no place without the daily exercise of justice,
The life-long learning of good.
Turn us, Creator, in the path of your steps.

EIGHTY-SIX

Preserve my soul for even I am holy.
I, too, am made in your image, under your mercy. I try to serve you.
Daily, I turn to you in prayer; for I trust in you.
Though I am poor in spirit, and needy in soul,
Beaten by proud people without, and chained by my own pride within,
Caught up in assemblies of violent people, and possessed by my own anger.

You, Creator, are full of compassion.
You are gracious, patient, radiant with mercy and truth.
To you, I lift up my soul.
For you are merciful to those who call upon you.
You have already delivered me from the lowest of hells.
Now, write my heart in humility and service.
Help me to walk in your truth.

EIGHTY-SEVEN

The roots of Creation are deep in the earth.
Its energies pulse in the flowing lavas at the center.
Rise in the holiness of the mountains.
The Creator loves the flowered fields and stark vistas,
More than all the dwellings and temples of people.
The Creator will remember those born in the soil,
Shall count those living in harmony with the earth.
All the songs of the soul rise from the springs of the earth.

EIGHTY-EIGHT

My life draws near to death. I am counted among the graves.
I have no strength. Am I to be loose among the dead?
Surrounded by waves of darkness, cut off from your hand?

I am alienated from my acquaintances. Illness shuts me off; I cannot go out.
All my senses are afflicted. Each day I have a new pain, or the same old pains.

Can you show wonders to the dead? Will the dead arise with praise,
Declare loving-kindness in the grave,
Sing of your faithfulness amidst destruction?
Shall your wonders be known in the dark,
Or your righteousness in the land of forgetfulness?

Creator, prevent my soul from dying.
Do not cast my spirit off, nor hide your truth from my face.
You know these terrors distract me. Lover and friend are drawing away.
I am afraid, yet, I am ready to die.

EIGHTY-NINE

I am here to make your faithfulness known to all generations.
I am a child of the agreements between people and God.
I am afraid because I am so close to your power,
A very small pillar of your faithfulness.

You, Creator, can quiet the sea and scatter civilizations.
You have made the earth in all its fullness,
And declared its meanings to our minds. Justice is the place of your seat.
Mercy and truth are your presence.

Blessed are people who know the sounds of joy,
Who walk in the edge of your light.
In simple goodness, they rejoice every day.
You are the glory of their strength. In you, we are mighty.
In neighborly service, we are chosen.
You anoint us in your truth, and guard us with faith and mercy.
We are members of your family. In love, we are children of God.

If we, or our children, forsake Creation's law, fail the commandments,
Live without goodness and love; then, we can expect Creation's discipline.
For, justice, in time, is done for every persons' deeds.
But God will never stop love, nor forsake faithfulness.
Creation will protect light in all the generations to come

When we have disregarded or mistaken our way and our work,
The covenants may seem void, The trust destroyed, God's love far away.
The days of youth do pass quickly. Shame covers each of us at some time.
Human wrath burns us all like fire. Does it burn in vain?
We live, but we also die, feel your loving-kindness, but also your reproach.

I am here to make your faithfulness known to all generations.
I am a very small pillar of your faithfulness.
I am still afraid, but close to your power.

Child's Grave:
Norway

NINETY

The Creator was the womb of the world, life's habitat before life began.
Vibrant now throughout the planets, enduring forever in its changing forms.

Human passion reflects Creation's energy,
Yet, people are consumed by their passions.
These energies turn us to destruction, carry us away like a flood,
Yet, call us also to return to God.

You, Creator, are forever, a thousand years is for you but a sleep.
But we are like the grass: in the morning, we grow up and flourish;
In the evening, we wither and are cut down.
For, we are consumed by the energies of life,
Troubled by anger, destroyed by hate.
Our secret sins dry us up, our excesses dull us in their fat,
Pride tightens our joints, envy blinds us to the simple truths.

For us, a life is seventy years.
If strength and fortune give us more, sorrow and labor come with the strength,
Tragedy and trials join with the good fortune.
So, teach us to live each of our days, that we may apply our hearts to wisdom.
This is your mercy, and we shall rejoice in it.
Then, even afflictions can be cherished, life's evils also be used for learning.

Let the beauty of the Creation, our God, be upon us,
And establish thou the work of our hands and hearts upon us.
Yes, the work of our hands and hearts, establish thou them.

NINETY-ONE

We dwell in the shadow of the Creator's name.
Creation gives us the refuge of love throughout the years of our lives,
We can save, nurture and honor the incredible light of being.
We can do much to satisfy existence,
Add fully our uniqueness to sanctify the earth and its people.

Creation delivers each of us from many traps.
We miss a multitude of tragedies,
Walk unafraid of much envy and violence, many terrors and storms.
Each living person knows the grace of not being destroyed,
Of seeing a multitude of evils and plagues,
And remaining untouched by most of them.

Keep us, Creator in your ways.
Bear us up so that we do not dash ourselves against the stones.
Shield us from the beasts without and the terrors within.
Set your love upon us, and help us to live your name.

Demon and Temple:
Thailand

NINETY-TWO

Any triumph I have will come through reflecting the Creation in the work I do.
To show loving-kindness every day is truly to give you thanks.
To remain faithful, even in the darkest nights, is fully to sing your praises.
With my ten fingers, and with every word of my mouth,
Upon the solemn harp of my heart,
May your deep thoughts and great works play.

When we are brutish, we shall know you not.
When we are foolish, we shall fail to understand.
Wickedness sometimes grows like the grass, and iniquity may flourish,
But only toward destruction. Enemies reflect our own desires.
If we would be exalted, we must anoint ourselves in freshness.
Not merely wait for you,
But live love and faithfulness every day and night of our lives.

Then, our desires will reflect your spirit,
And not the tragic adventures of the wicked.
Then, we may flourish like the palm tree and the cedar.
Plant yourselves in the garden of God.
Bring forth fruit even in old age, and flourish each of your days.
The Creation is a great tree, and each of us can be its root and branch.

NINETY-THREE

The world has order, meaning and stability. Its ways are strongly founded.
Creativity moves on in its eternal paths. Chaos remains:
Floods wash great cities away; many dark dreams come true.
But order, meaning and stability are stronger.
Creativity in all its majesty and strength is far more powerful.
Creativity moves on in its eternal paths.

NINETY-FOUR

Vengeance may belong to God, but it should not be a part of human character.
God may render justice to the proud.
It is for us to do good and practice mercy in the Earth and with one another.
How long shall we speak harshly and fill the air with boasting?
Will we always afflict our heritage?
Remain careless of the needy, suspicious of strangers,
Be brutish and foolish forever?

You think that God does not hear and see?
The Creator that placed the ear, and formed the eye.
Cannot the creator correct? Does not the teacher have knowledge?
The Creator knows our finitude, the experimental nature of human thought.
Blessed are those people who also know their limits,
Who realize that their truths are only hypotheses.
Such people can begin to learn the laws of God.

This is the blessing of God's chastening power.
Humility gives rest from the days of adversity,
And allows us to comprehend our inheritance.
By leaving vengeance and cosmic justice to God,
Our souls have time to discover peace. Creation's mercy supports us all,
Giving us the comforts of the spirit in the multitude of our thoughts.

NINETY-FIVE

Make a joyful noise to creation. Make a joyful noise with psalms.
Creation's greatness is far beyond all rulers.
In creation are the deep places of the earth, and the strength of the hills,
The vast seas and the deserts. All alike bow before their maker.
Hear, again, Creation's voice, Harden not your heart. Do not provoke chaos.
Remember our ancestors, Who tempted, proved, and saw.
Must each generation take its forty years in the wilderness?
Err in their hearts and grieve their God?
See what has been taught in the past, and enter into the peace of God.

NINETY-SIX

Sing to Creation a new song. Celebrate salvation daily.
Declare wonders, banish fears, worship no idols.
Worship honor and majesty wherever you find them.
For strength and beauty joined together are the living sanctuaries of God.

By your lives, give God glory and strength. Each of you can be a vital offering,
A pillar of God's sanctuary. Worship by creating and nurturing beauty,
By practicing and preserving goodness. Support the earth and live in its spirit.
Do justice to your neighbors, and who is not your neighbor?

The seas roar; the fields wave in gladness.
The trees reach up, and every creature has its song. Will you do less?
All your days are spread before creation.
God sings in every truthful thought and caring deed.

NINETY-SEVEN

We are a multitude of islands adrift in the ocean of God.
Darkness and complexity surround us,
Yet goodness and truth remain the essence of life.
Some of us serve idols.
Others boast of themselves.
Each person must decide what is to be served, and do those things.

God seems far away; so, preserve us with caring friends.
Light spreads from righteous action, gladness glows from the upright heart.
Rejoice and give thanks for the common grace of our days.
We are islands together in the deep and blissful ocean of God.

Japanese Garden:
Portland, Oregon

NINETY-EIGHT

Sing to Creation a new song. Its truths can be imagined by everyone.
Pluck the harps, chant the psalms, blow the horns.
Let our human voices roar like the sea,
And the people grow in praise like the evolving earth.
Emotions are our floods; Let us clap our hands. People be joyful together,
Just as the hills stand side by side in peace before the Creator.

NINETY-NINE

There is something terrible about the Creation: it is so vast and endless.
It moves the Earth and reigns on high, judges both the great and humble,
Is the source of all strength, the endless rush of power, the cosmic dark.

Yet, people find Creation equitable. Many prophets have called Its name.
It spoke to Moses in the cloudy pillar. Kept Its word to many,
Its ordinances for eternity. It may answer you.
It is our faith that Creation does justice to our inventions, and forgives us.
Faith embraces the mercy behind the terror, the order beyond the power.

ONE HUNDRED

Sing a joyful song to the world.
For each of you is a living tradition.
Serve life with gladness.
Share yourselves gracefully.
The world is a holy place.
We are presented with the gift of life,
And we should serve life with truth and good will.
Be thankful, and not too small to praise.
Our lives are worthy of blessing and of joy.
Every hour contains goodness, mercy mediates each day,
And truth endures to all generations.

ONE HUNDRED ONE

I shall behave myself wisely, and walk in my home with a kind heart.
Neither shall I accustom myself to evil, nor lose myself in criticism.
My way will not be to force or flaunt, neither to join the slanderers,
Nor to tarry with the wicked.
I shall not need to be haughty, my heart pounding with pride.
My eyes will follow the faithful.
Each day I shall try to do good, and to live without evil.
Deceit will not dwell in my house.
Liars shall not remain with me.
Help me to overcome my weaknesses, and to build upon my strengths.

ONE HUNDRED TWO

Hear my prayer, God, for I am ill.
Do not hide your face from me,
For I am in trouble. I need your help.
My heart is beaten, and I am withered like the grass.
I forget to eat or drink.
I am like a pelican lost at sea, an owl in the bright desert,
A baby sparrow wavering on a housetop.
I have eaten ashes like bread, and mingled my drink with weeping.
My days are declining shadows. My nights are the rustling of dead leaves.
But you, God, shall endure forever, and your memory into all generations.
Your name will be strong, your mercy widespread,
And many will be the children of your spirit.
Regard now, my destitute spirit.
Remember always the prayers of those in trouble.
Hear the groaning of the prisoners; free those that are appointed to death.
My strength has weakened as the years passed.
Now, my days are short.

God, in you, my days are throughout the generations.
From the beginning of time, and the birth of the world,
Beings have died and events passed, but you endure.
People get old, like garments, and you change us for new clothes,
But you remain the same, and the children of your spirit will continue.
Their seed will grow and blossom, endlessly, throughout the future.

ONE HUNDRED THREE

Bless the Creator.
Do not forget the benefits of creation.
Creation heals every disease of the soul,
Redeems us repeatedly from destruction,
Crowns us with loving-kindness and tender mercies.
Satisfies our senses with good things,
So that our days are renewed in eager youthfulness.
The Creator is merciful and gracious.
Does not deal with us by the weight of our sins,
Nor rewards us according to our inadequacies.

As large as the universe, so large is the mercy of God.
Removing our failures and frailties, pitying us as a parent does her erring child,
The Creator remembers our finitude, sees our limits.

As a flower of the field, we grow, flourish, and die.
The wind passes over, and we are gone.
Our home knows us no more.
But the mercy of God is everlasting.
Those who do their human duty, and live full of love and mercy,
Do the Creator's pleasure.

Butchart Garden:
Victoria, British Columbia, Canada

ONE HUNDRED FOUR

Creation, you are clothed in honor and majesty.
Light is your garment; heavens spread your splendid curtains.
Deep oceans make chambers for your leisure,
And you walk upon the wings of the wind.
Your face is in the flaming fire.
Your voices are the songs of the universe.

It is you who laid the foundations of the Earth,
Who created deep waters and chastened them with mountains,
Who put springs among the hills, and rivers in the valleys
So that every living being might quench their thirst.
By you, the birds sing, the grass grows.
Food is brought forth for all the living.
In some place every being finds a home:
Whether it is the stork in the fir tree, or the wild goats on the rocks,
Whales in the oceans, lions of the plains.
The world is large enough for all.
You have given to each in its seasons.
The earth is satisfied with the harvest of your deeds.

Human beings also arise with the sun and go forth to their work.
They see the greatness of the earth, and enjoy the seasons of time.
The wines of life make their hearts glad.
Its oils make their bodies shine,
And its breads strengthen their hearts.
You open your hands, and we are filled with good.
You hide your face, and we are troubled.
Take away our breath, and we die and return to dust.
When your spirit goes forth,
Beings are created, and the face of the earth is renewed.
Oh, this meditation on God is sweet!
While I have my being, I shall sing.

Boats and Skyline:
Hong Kong, China

ONE HUNDRED FIVE

Glory in the Creator's holy name.
Make known God's deeds among all people.
What seed God planted in Abraham, and raised in Jacob.
How that seed spread from one nation to another,
From a single seed to a great harvest.
How the sheaves of Joseph went forth to Egypt in bondage,
And came forth with Moses as the bread of heaven.

For God remembers the promise
And confirms the works of joy, and the passions of gladness.
Now, we are the inheritors of this covenant,
The new harvests of this ancient seed.
May we observe the promise and keep the laws.
Oh, Creator, let us grow in your praise.

ONE HUNDRED SIX

We have been as mistaken as our ancestors.
We, too, have committed injustice and have worshipped falsely.
Many times they did not understand the revelations given to them.
We are, as often, blind to the important events and insights of our lives.

We are like Israel in the wilderness.
They did not understand the greatness of your mercy.
They soon forgot the miracles of the Red Sea and the desert.
Amidst all those miracles, alone with God in the desert,
They lusted after forbidden flesh and false rituals.
God gave them their desires, but also leanness of soul.
Only the presence of a few people of integrity
Saved the whole nation from just destruction.
Most failed to believe God's words, or to accept fully the promises of the land.

We also seem tempt condemnation.
Why do we provoke pain and resist creativity?
We have shed innocent blood on a scale unknown in ancient times.
The temptations are even greater now to serve false idols.
People still sacrifice their children to tyranny or oppression.
We, too, are defiled by our own works, and go whoring with our inventions.
We, too, turn our backs on wisdom
And are brought low for our failures of integrity.
Yet, God has pity, and preserves us.

The Creator is waiting for us to break our self-made bonds,
To outgrow our inner torments and mutual pain.
The Creator is waiting for us to surmount our leanness of soul,
Waiting for us to fulfill the promises between God and her people.

ONE HUNDRED SEVEN

Praise the Creator for the fabulous works of the future,
For new generations of children.

Even the redeemed have wandered in solitary ways with no stopping place.
Even the purest souls have known hunger and thirst.
Many sit in darkness, even in the shadow of death,
Bound to affliction because they, too, have rebelled against God,
Have condemned the counsels of mercy and wisdom.
God satisfies the longing soul, fills the searching soul with goodness.

Fools, by their cruelties and apathy, are afflicted.
Their souls abhor growth, and draw near to death.
In the storms of life, our souls are melted,
Confounded by the wonders and terrors of the deep.
Like sailors, we reel in life's storms and are at our wit's end.
God makes the waves still, and quiets the heart.

Seekers build cities, and the strong sow fields,
While royalty and pride lives to reap contempt.
They wander in wilderness where there is no way.
Many are brought low through oppression, affliction and sorrow,
Most are brought low by themselves.
Yet the poor are blessed with children, the good with vision,
And the wise know the love of God.
Everyone, in their times, cry out,
And God makes the waves still, and quiets the heart.

Praise the Creator for the fabulous works of the future,
For new generations of children.

Family:
Kashmir, India

ONE HUNDRED EIGHT

Our hearts are fixed.
Though you cast us off like dirt from your shoes,
We will lean on your help, and valiantly attempt your will.
We will wake early in your praise; your mercy is great.
Embrace your power; for its sparks were promised to the human spirit.
Though we are troubled from every side, through God we shall do valiantly.

ONE HUNDRED NINE

What shall be done with those who do not remember to show mercy,
Who persecute the poor and needy, who even destroy the broken-hearted?
It is tempting to seek curses against them,
To reflect their wickedness in our mouths,
Using their lies and having hate of our own,
With prayers, in despair, for vengeance.

There are many adversaries of love:
Rewarding evil for good and hatred for care.
These diabolical powers are strong.
Often, they cause good people to seek vengeance,
To try force and work violence, tempt curses from the merciful,
Blind hatred from the wise, deceit from the truthful.

As we or anyone loves cursing; so, let their curses return to them.
As we or anyone forgets the delight of blessing, may blessings move far away.
Creator, we are wounded by the injustices of the world,
Feel persecuted by people who fight against us without cause.
Preserve us from the temptation to return hate for hate,
Blind rage and angry curses, instead of the mercy and blessings of your light.

Let us stand at the right hand of the poor, and attempt to save the condemned.
Make us be ashamed to curse, but brave enough to bless.
Let the children of your spirit rejoice in their works.

ONE HUNDRED TEN

You are a servant of God forever.
Always, you may be asked to be the Creator's right hand;
So, discipline yourself in the midst of all temptations.
People will work with you in the days of your power,
If morning reflects from your face, and youthful truth radiates from your spirit.
God's energy may work through you to loosen tyrannies,
Bring light to places of ignorance, growth even to the dying.
Servant, drink of the brook of God's grace as you go.
Thereby, you will be upright, and God will be glad.

ONE HUNDRED ELEVEN

Let us use our whole hearts in the active practice of praise,
In living the Creator's love.
God's work is to give lasting pleasure.
It is honorable and glorious because it is gracious and compassionate.
Living in this spirit, the heritages of all people are open to us.
Our work can be true and merciful.
We shall have sustenance, and our deeds will endure.
Respect for the awesome realities of life is the beginning of wisdom.
Living by the best of natural and human laws
Is the crux of the covenant between people and God.

ONE HUNDRED TWELVE

Unto the upright arises light even in darkness.
An upright person is gracious, full of compassion, has integrity.
She does favors, and lends her skills and resources to others.
Yet, she guides her own affairs with discretion.
She is not terrified by evil tidings for her heart is sure,
And she trusts in the Creator.
She shares herself with those truly in need.
While her desires will come to pass, the desires of others may perish.

ONE HUNDRED THIRTEEN

Praise the Creation in all its multitude of names
And love those who serve its spirit.
From daybreak to twilight, do God's work and love its creations.
Who is like the Creator?
Those who open themselves to reality,
Who seek God's spirit in every day, creature, and circumstance,
Who nurture, enhance, even help to create God's work in the world.
These are royalty among humanity.
Such work has all the potency of Earth, and the joy of the Creator.

ONE HUNDRED FOURTEEN

From many peoples of strange languages, God would have one human family.
Every home could be a sanctuary, and all lands should share the peace of God.
When the peoples are gathered and united, the sea may flee,
The mountains skip like rams; then, such miracles will be of lasting value.
Then, the Earth will no longer tremble in fear at human violence,
But dance in joy, as these spiritual companions reflect the light of God.

ONE HUNDRED FIFTEEN

You, God, are mercy and love within us, truth and light among us.
Yet, you are cosmic and all encompassing,
Who has done and will do whatever you please.

We know that idols are but passions personified,
The seductive fantasies of human hands and minds.
Idols may have mouths, but they will not speak, eyes, but they cannot see,
Ears, but they are deaf.
We can give them hands, but they will remain idle.
We may invest them with power, even of life and death over us,
But they have no power of their own.
They can neither walk, speak, nor do, except by our self-destroying passions.
Those that make idols become like them, as do those that trust in them.

We would trust in virtue, in the living God.
We want to believe in the powers of mercy and truth.
Our faith is that the world, and our lives, make sense:
Not in our fits of anger or desolation, but through our years of service,
Our relationships of love, care, and understanding.
The universe demands awe, as does the glorious, evolving Earth,
Even the flourishing children of human culture demand respect.
And awe and respect surges out of everyone who has the eyes to see,
The minds to grasp, and the courage to love.

All this is God's.
Yet God seems to have given us, humans, some stewardship for the Earth;
So, let us praise God, not in death, but by our deeds and our days.

ONE HUNDRED SIXTEEN

I am able to love because I have been loved,
To be grateful because I have been blessed by grace,
To listen because someone had the patience to hear me.

Sorrows of death surrounded me, my body was full of pain,
My soul tracked by despair; then, I called: 'God, preserve this simple person.'
You were gracious and merciful to me. You delivered my soul from death,
My eyes from their tears, and my feet from falling.
Yet, in my haste and ignorance, I cried:
'All people are liars, uncaring, without love or grace.' I was wrong.

Give me the strength to offer the sacrifice of joy.
Teach me the discipline of thanksgiving.
Make me strong enough to live the daily worship of honest acts of goodness..
May I reflect the glory of God, which I, myself, have seen,
In the simple integrity of ordinary people.

I was able to love because I have been loved,
To be grateful because I have been blessed by grace,
To listen because someone had the patience to hear me.

ONE HUNDRED SEVENTEEN

Praise God all nations, praise the Creator every person.
For mercy flows through us like a river, and truth encompasses us like the air.
Praise the Creator.

ONE HUNDRED EIGHTEEN

God's mercy endures. The Creator set me in a large place.
I shall not fear. What can anyone do to me when God takes my part?
There are those that help me, and the Creator seems to put my goals
Even into the lives of those that dislike me.

God's mercy endures.
It is better to trust in the Creator
Than to put too much confidence in any person,
Even in leaders or prophets.
We are all members of nations, act like bees in their hives,
But thorns and fire are among the citizen's rewards,
And every nation is eventually destroyed.

God's mercy endures. I shall do justice in praise of the Creator.
I shall tell how the stone of my soul, which the nations had refused,
Has become a cornerstone for my people.
The Creator has chastened me sorely, yet, has not given me over to death.
Creation is my strength and my song.

God's mercy endures.
This is the day which Creation has made.
We shall rejoice, and be glad in it.
Come to one another in the Creator's name and the creative spirit.
Share the spirit of Creation in your homes,
Keep the Creator's flame burning in your hearts.
God's mercy endures forever.

Arch:
St. Louis, Missouri

Psalm One Hundred Nineteen has twenty-two sections, each traditionally headed by a different abbreviated name, whose meanings have been lost for most people. This Psalm is a book of psalms in itself, reflecting the many voices of praise, standing as a vigorous lesson about the vitality and complexity of Creation's law. I have chosen to connect the twenty-two sections with well-known characters from the Old Testament. This added levels of difficulty and required an additional year. I hope the extra effort helps to fulfill the original intention. In a single Psalm their whole tradition is revealed, the grand complexity of Creation's laws.

EVE (verses 1-8)

Blessed are those undefiled by their own actions,
Whose life paths follow the laws of creation.
Blessed are those who preserve the virtues given to them,
Who seek God with their whole hearts, yet, also, surmount the habits of evil.

Oh, that my ways were in harmony with your principles;
Then, I would not be ashamed, I could respect myself,
And honor your commandments by my actions.
Living praise is uprightness of heart, learning the true distinctions.
Forsake me not utterly; for I shall try to live your truths.

ADAM (verses 9-16)

How is a young man purified? By heeding the words of God.
I sought the Creator with my heart,
But I wandered away from creation's daily disciplines.
Yet, I kept its truths in my heart; so, my errors did not destroy me.

Creation, teach me the way.
With my lips, I declare for you, but my body is weak.
Though we lose the riches of paradise,
Your words remaining in our hearts are their equal in value.
May we meditate upon them,
And have respect for the disciplines of living.
I will not forget your word.

CAIN (verses 17-24)

Mine is the bounty of life:
I am allowed to behold wondrous things.
Open my eyes that I may see my own powers for good among your miracles.
Hide not virtue from me, for I remain a stranger on the Earth.

My soul breaks for the longing I have for my brother.
You have rebuked me for my worship,
And cursed me for my indignation.
Remove from me this useless condemnation.
For, I have meditated upon your way, and my children are your delight.

ABEL (verses 25-32)

My soul divides the dust, please quicken my effects.
You honored my ways by death,
Now help me to understand the meaning of my dying.
Perhaps my soul melted of its own heavy righteousness?
Maybe your affirmation of my ritual alone was a lie?

I tried to be truthful,
Just as now I am trying to accept the reality you have given me.
Do not put my name to shame.
Let your commandments enlarge my brother's heart; for he lives.

METHUSELAH AND OTHER GIANTS IN THE EARTH (verses 33-40)

Teach us, Creator, the way reality works, and we shall keep it to the end.
Give us understanding, and we shall live it with our whole beings.
Command us the paths; let these be our delights.
Incline us not to wealth and power, but to the ways of the spirit.
Guide us away from vanity.

Stabilize your laws for us; for the flux of life still fills us with fear.
We do not want to waste away reproaching ourselves.
We want to live realistically, related to your spirit.
We long after your ways, but strengthen our practices.

NOAH (verses 41-48)

Let mercy come also to me and my flock
Even your salvation according to the word. For, I trust your words.
Give me a part in this truth: for, I have hope.

It will be my word to try to keep the law.
Then, we can walk at liberty, seeking your truths,
Speak before anyone and not be ashamed. Your laws will be our love.
We shall lift our hands to their promise and meditate upon their fruits.

HAGAR (verses 49-56)

Remember, you have caused me to hope. In my affliction, this is my comfort.
The proud have me in derision, yet I have not stopped practicing the law.
I have considered your past justice and have comforted myself.

Some wicked do flourish; many flaunt the law,
Horror does sometimes take hold of me.
Yet, even then, the laws remain my song, the food of my pilgrimage.
Through every storm, the candlelight of the laws have kept me,
Have caused me, yet, to hope.

SARAI (verses 57-64)

You are my portion, Creator. I have entreated your favor with my whole heart.
I thought on your ways and turned to your testimonies.
I made haste, not delaying to keep your will.

The bands of the wicked have robbed me, but I have not forgotten you.
At midnight, I rise to give you thanks.
I am a companion for all those who feel your power and live in your spirit.
The Earth, Creator, is full of mercy.

ABRAHAM (verses 65-72)

You have dealt well with me, God,
But my good fortune afflicted my understanding,
Even your commandments weakened my power to decide in crisis.
Teach me good judgment and wisdom.
For by keeping my word, I was led astray;
I was tempted to sacrifice my son on the altars of yesterday.

It is too simple to make future generations
Bear the burdens of past guilt and pride,
So easy to force the future into molds of my own strife.
You are good and do good.
The proud have forged another lie against us both.
For you would not ask fathers to sacrifice their sons,
But rather ask both, perhaps, to sacrifice ourselves
So that grandchildren would live,
And the seeds among us all be blessed.

ISSAC (verses 72-80)

Your hands have made me, Father God.
This world has fashioned my understanding.
I see its fire and wood, but where are its lambs of sacrifice?
Am I the lamb, and are we each the sacrifice of unrequited dreams of yours,
Of pain and grief divinely deep?

Does faithfulness tempt fathers with their sons,
Ask blood of children, to grow old?
There must be mercy on your face, and justice in your hands
Or fear would bind us all to nothingness,
And I would lie dead upon the mountain of my father's dreams.
Oh, let our hearts be sound.

JOB (verses 81-88)

My soul faints waiting for salvation, but I do still believe in you, God.
My eyes fail seeking your word, when will you comfort me?
I have become as useless as a bottle filled with smoke,
Yet I do not forget your laws. How long must I live?

Will you ever do justice to my persecutors?
The proud set traps for me perverting the spirit of the laws.
The laws themselves are just, but I am persecuted unjustly.
Help me, Creator!
I am almost consumed by life, yet I have lived your truths.
I need your loving-kindness now to remain a symbol of your truth.

ESAU (verses 89-96)

Forever, Creator, your truths continue, Your justice abides.
Your creation is made forever. Everything serves you and your plan.

Unless your truths had been my delight I would have perished in my affliction.
I shall not forget your justices for I need them to survive.
The wicked have carefully planned my despair,
But I still consider the facts of each new day.
I have seen the end of all perfection, but your laws are exceedingly broad.

JACOB (verses 97-104)

Oh how I love your law!
How glorious it has shaped my fate.
It has made me wiser than my enemies,
Given me better understanding than any teacher,
Made me more cunning than all of the ancestors.
Surely, I must have fulfilled its precepts?

I have retraced my steps from every evil path.
I have been a good student of your opportunities.
How sweet does success taste.
My whole being is ecstatic!
Through reality I have learned; therefore, I hate every false turn.

JOSEPH (verses 105-112)

Your word is a lamp for my feet and a light on my path.
I have promised, and I will do your justice.
Though I have been afflicted, teach me the truth
And allow me to share your gifts freely.

My soul is continually in my hand, but I do not forget your grace.
Though the wicked have caught me in their traps, I do not need to live revenge.
Your testimonies are my heritage forever; they are the rejoicing of my heart.
Put your laws in my heart.
Give me the courage to act until the end.

AARON (verses 113-120)

I have vain thoughts, but I do love Creation's law.
It is my hiding place and my shield. The law is my hope in this world.
Depart from me, evil temptations,
For I shall keep the commandments of my Creator.
Let me live, and not be ashamed to have hope.

If you stop me, I shall be safe; then, my respect can be real.
Error and deceit will be walked over and blown away, like the dust.
Oh, let me love the laws enough.
My flesh trembles in fear of your judgments.

MOSES (verses 121-128)

I have held power and done justice, leave me not alone.
Keep your promises of good.
Do not let the proud oppress the law.
My eyes fail looking for the promised land,
Waiting for the fulfillment of your promises.
Be merciful with me and mine, teach us the truth.
We do serve you; give us some satisfaction.
It is time for you, Creator, to work.

The law is made empty in our hearts by the ceaseless passing of the years.
I love your commandments above gold, cattle, or land.
I celebrate your laws concerning all things, and I hate every other way.

RUTH (verses 129-136)

Your testimonies are wonderful; my soul cherishes them with gladness
Their appearance gives light.
In time, it gives understanding to the simple people.
I have panted, with open mouth, for your ways.

Give me, with mercy, your grace,
As you have done in the past to those who loved you.
Order my steps, do not let iniquity control me.
Deliver me from the oppressions of other people,
Make your face shine upon me as I serve you.
It makes me cry a river, that people do not keep your law.

SAMSON (verses 137-144)

Creator, I know you are the good, and your judgements sure.
But my zeal has consumed me because even my intimates have lost your ways.
These ways are pure, and I love them, yet, now, I am weak and despised.
Still, I do not forget your ways.

The truth is the law. Goodness will endure.
Though trouble and anguish have seized me,
Yet your ways are my deepest courage.
Give me understanding,
And I shall empower your truths.

ELIJAH (verses 145-152)

You are near, Creator, and all your truth is real.
I have cried with my whole heart, sought salvation with all of my being.
Yet, our very hopes prevent the dawning of the morning.
Your words in our mouths prolong the night watches.
Many draw near provoked and planning mischief. We are far from your law.

Oh, Creator, your loving-kindness is as necessary as the rain,
After seven years of unremitting Sun.
I have faith that all that is said will come true.
But let your truth shine now, and open the door between us.

SAUL (verses 153-160)

Consider my pain and deliver me, for I have not forgotten the law.
Take my defense, keep your promises.
Wickedness pushes you away,
Yet your tenderness can be great.

My enemies and persecutions surround me, and I still speak on your behalf.
I have seen my friends turn against me and fail their promises to me,
Yet I love your truths because of your loving-kindness for me.
I know that goodness will, somehow, always endure.

DAVID (verses 161-168)

Princes have persecuted me unfairly, but I stand in awe of you.
I rejoice in your reality as a person discovering countless wealth.
I abhor falsity, and I love truth.

Seven times a day do I sing praises,
Seven times seven, do I befriend your people.
Great peace is there in the love of the law.
All my ways are before you, judge them with tenderness,
May your love strike me like a stone.

HUMANITY (verses 169-175)

Please hear me, Creation.
Give me understanding.
Let the best of these words, put in your mouth, be true.

I shall utter praise but, please, teach me the law.
I speak on your behalf, but guide me in the truth.
Let my soul live, may reality be good to me.
I have often gone astray.
I feel lost from the truth.
Please hear me, God, and seek your humbled servant.

ONE HUNDRED TWENTY

We cry. Does the Creator hear?
Does God listen to distress, or only to praise?
Does the Creator hear lies, or only the truth?
Deliver our souls, O God, from lying lips and from a deceitful tongue.

What shall be given for lies? What shall be done to deceit?
Woe is me that I rest among role players,
And dwell in a civilization based on cunning.
My soul lives surrounded by strife; yet, I live for peace, praise, and for truth.
Deliver me from lies and from distress built upon deceit.

ONE HUNDRED TWENTY-ONE

I will lift up my eyes to the Creator of heaven and earth, who is my help?
God can hold the brave firm to their challenge, and protect the child in slumber.
Has God not preserved Israel all these years?
The sun shines, but does not burn us up.
The moon moves the tides, but the oceans do not wash us away.
God can preserve us from all evil, and will preserve our souls.
The Creator preserved our going out,
And will create our coming in from this time forever more.

My Son Sleeping:
Paramus, New Jersey

ONE HUNDRED TWENTY-TWO

I was glad when they said to me: Let us go into the house of Creation.
This is the great promise: That every foot can stand within the gates of God.
For each of us, Jerusalem exists.
There is an ideal community,
Where our inheritance and our visions give thanks together,
Where judgment and experience rest in each other's arms.

Pray for the peace of this universal vision.
May all prosper that love it.
Make peace with your past, building prosperity for your present.
Let us all find peace together.
For if God's house is to be built, or to endure,
We must seek the good of our neighbors and our friends.

ONE HUNDRED TWENTY-THREE

God, I feel bad about myself.
My soul is filled with the scorn of those at ease,
And with the contempt of the proud.
Have mercy upon me, God, for I am exceedingly full of contempt for myself.

Yet, I still have courage to lift my eyes to you, even up to the heavens.
I seek your hands as my master, your eyes as my mistress.
God, I wait for your mercy to reawaken my own sense of worth and purpose.
Let me also lift my soul to the heavens.

ONE HUNDRED TWENTY-FOUR

If the Creator had not been at our side,
Could we have escaped the snares of life?
It seemed that all the world had arisen against us,
But we were not swallowed by their wrath,
Nor washed away by the floods of the Earth.
If the Creator had not been at our side,
The fiery wrath and proud waters would have overwhelmed our souls.

Blessed be the Creator who has not given us as prey.
Our souls have escaped like birds from the traps of the hunter.
The snares are broken, and we are free.
Our help is in the Creator who made heaven and earth.

ONE HUNDRED TWENTY-FIVE

The good are like the mountains:
Unmoved by ordinary turmoils, lasting, practically, forever.
God encompasses the good in Creation's spirit.

Wicked people may strive and struggle with the good,
But the good will not sink down, nor even be lost in the iniquities of the wicked.
Many will turn aside into crooked ways,
Yet Creation may lead them forth again into peace,
While the good are blessed by the daily living of truth,
And the common practice of right ways.
Do good, O God, unto those that be good,
And to them that are upright in their hearts.

ONE HUNDRED TWENTY-SIX

When we became, again, a free people, It seemed we must be dreaming;
Then, our mouths filled with laughter, and our voices with song.
We had said for so long: the Creator had done great things for them.
Now, we could say: the Creator has done great things for us, and we are glad.

God, help all people to be free; turn the tides forever toward freedom.
May others, like us, who sowed in tears, reap in joy.
Every person bears the precious seeds of life and spirit.
Existence may be tragic, but rejoicing, and the fruits of one's labor,
Could be harvested by every person.

ONE HUNDRED TWENTY-SEVEN

Children are the house of God.
Their integrity are the walls and the streets of your cities.
It is vain for you to rise up early, to sit up late, or to eat the bread of sorrow,
For God gave the children liberty with their breath.

Children are the heritage of the Creator, and the greatest reward for any person.
Children are the hands of human might.
Happy is the person whose life is filled with children.
Parents shall seldom be ashamed of existence,
And can speak with their enemies in peace.

Children:
Israel

ONE HUNDRED TWENTY-EIGHT

Blessed is everyone who practices
The integrity of love and the discipline of justice.
They walk in God's way.
They will eat the labor of their hands,
Are happy in themselves, and at peace with their neighbors.
Their best dreams will come true, and they will harvest their fondest hopes.
Such as these are blessed in their awe of nature, and their respect for truth.
This is the elusive fear of God: the integrity of love and the discipline of justice.
Its practitioners may live to see their children's children, and will find peace.

ONE HUNDRED TWENTY-NINE

Many times, I have been afflicted since my youth.
Israel is also crisscrossed with the plows and the swords of many nations,
Yet, both I and Israel, have prevailed despite all our adversities.
Justice happens: ignorance is confounded, hate turned back.
Wickedness dies like grass on the rooftops, withering before it grows up.
Evil brings neither harvests nor satisfaction.
Blessings are evoked by right living.

ONE HUNDRED THIRTY

Out of my depths I have cried to thee, O God.
Please hear my cries and give hope to my supplications.
If God condemns each doer of evil, who shall be left standing?
But beyond fear, there is in God, forgiveness.
Thus, my soul waits upon the Creator, and in Its word I do hope,
My soul waits for the Creator,
More, even, than those that watch for the morning;
For God, alone, can bring light to the depths of my soul.

ONE HUNDRED THIRTY-ONE

Creator, my soul is that of a weaned child.
My heart is not haughty, nor my eyes lofty.
I do not assert myself in cosmic matters, nor in other things too high for me.
I am learning to quiet myself,
As the weaned child learns to begin its own care.
As our hope is in you; so, also, we must learn to care for ourselves.
God is our mother, but we must be as weaned children.

ONE HUNDRED THIRTY-TWO

Creator, remember David's particular affliction?
He swore not to go home, nor to sleep, until he had found you a home,
Or discovered your habitation.

Many are so afflicted, crying in their varied voices:
Arise, Creator, rest in my holy place,
Let my priests be clothed with righteousness, let my saints shout for joy.
For the sake of my ancient heritage, do not turn your face away from me.

People see truth in their past, and hope they are its fruits.
Children are called upon to keep the ancient laws;
For, according to their scriptures, God has chosen them, and their place.

Thus, God blesses the believer. Satisfying the poor with bread,
The priests with salvation, the saints with joy.
Each believer is an inheritor of David, somewhat ashamed by the light of truth,
Yet, anointed, like Israel, with the crown of God's concern.

Mosque:
Iran

ONE HUNDRED THIRTY-THREE

Behold, how good and how pleasant it is for people to dwell together in unity.
Love's precious ointment of life, flowing from minds to words, to all our beings.
Like the dew upon the mountains, is human unity in love.
This is Creation's blessing upon us.
This is our life forevermore.

ONE HUNDRED THIRTY-FOUR

You stand in the house of Creation, lift your hands to make God's sanctuary.
Serve the living spirit, maker of heaven and earth,
You must also bless Creation.
God requires your help.

ONE HUNDRED THRITY-FIVE

Sing pleasant praises to the Creator
Has God not chosen our people?
Is not your God the high God?
Whatsoever the Creation wills It is done in heaven and on Earth,
In the seas and on the depths of the land.
God's will evolving on the Earth as vapors to rain, rain to rivers,
Rivers to the sea, and seas back into the sky again.

Has God not also done wonders among us?
Who smote great nations and slew mighty kings, shook Egypt from its pride,
And gave Israel as our heritage?
Creation endures and has mercy for Its servants.

The idols of others are the works of human hands.
They have mouths, but do not speak, eyes, but are blind,
Are deaf, despite their ears, and are without breath in their throats.
They that make them are like them; so, is everyone that trusts in them.
Respect the living God, and praise the Creator with your life.

ONE HUNDRED THIRTY-SIX

The Creator is goodness, and Its mercy endures forever.
Stretching out the earth above the waters, creating the light.
The sun rules by day, the moon and stars at night.
For Its mercy endures forever.

The Creator brought out Israel from Egypt, divided the sea,
Punished the Egyptians, led Israel through the wilderness,
And gave them their land of promise, for Its mercy endures forever.

God who remembers us in low estate redeems us from our enemies,
Gives food to all flesh.
Give thanks to the Creator
For its mercy endures forever.

ONE HUNDRED THIRTY-SEVEN

By the rivers of Babylon,
There we all sit down, and weep, remembering the past.
We hang our harps on the willows of those streams.
Those who have carried us to this day require of us, a song.
How can we sing our songs in a strange land?

If I forget my heritage, wither my hands.
Seal my mouth, if my past is not a great joy.
Help me never to forget the destruction of so much that we cherished.
How, yet, those memories wreak my soul.

Despite the pain of memory, let me pluck my harp by the strange streams.
May I sing the best of my past to my children in this new land.

ONE HUNDRED THIRTY-EIGHT

I praise you with my whole heart.
Before any other gods, I shall sing your praises.
I still return to your holy temple:
Your loving-kindness and your truth, for these empower your name.

When I cry, you answer me, strengthening my soul.
Even kings will praise you when they feel your virtue; for your glory is great.
Though your are high, yet you respect the lowly,
And stand far away from the proud.
Though I walk in the midst of trouble, you revive me,
Dispelling the wrath of enemies, reaching out to save me.

Creator, you perfect the essence of each of us,
While having mercy about our concerns.
You do not forsake the work of your hands.

ONE HUNDRED THIRTY-NINE

You have searched and known me.
You know my weaknesses and my strengths;
You know my thoughts from the beginning.
You surround my work and my rest,
Are acquainted with all my ways.
The Creator knows all, controls past and future,
Is the hand upon our passing presents.
Such knowledge is beyond us humans.
We cannot attain it.
Why try to flee God?

God is the wings of the morning and the shadows of night.
Every wave of the sea, every ray of light is the Creator.
God covers our wombs and holds the reins.
We are fearfully and wonderfully made.
Marvelous are your works,
And the soul does know right.

When I was made in secret, you knew my substance, all my curious parts,
You knew I was imperfect, but you gave me also my unity and uniqueness.
Your precious thoughts are alive in us: as many as the grains of ocean sands.
When we awake, you are still with us.

Creation, overcome wickedness.
Help me depart from bloody people.
I would not speak evil, nor use your name in vain.
I am grieved at rebellion and hate; let me practice justice and love.
Search me and know my heart.
Try me and test my deeds.
Evaporate the wickedness from my soul, and lead me in eternal ways.

ONE HUNDRED FORTY

Deliver me from evil persons.
Preserve me from violent persons
Who imagine mischief in their hearts, and continually prepare for war.
They spread poison with their words, converting the rest of us to their ways.
Their pride easily seduces all of us.

I would simplify myself to goodness: not giving way to evil acts,
Nor allowing violence to be justified.
I would confound the mischief makers.
Humble them in their own darkness.
Burn them with their own wrath,
And allow the violent to destroy themselves.
Ours is the cause of the afflicted; we seek the rights of the poor.
Only the upright can look steadily into the eyes of life,
And into the hearts of one another.

ONE HUNDRED FORTY-ONE

God, I cry in haste, accept my simple prayer as worship,
My stark gesture as a sacrifice.
Guard and govern my speech; for I am tempted to practice wicked words.
Keep me from their fascination.
Let the truth hit me, and rightness govern me.
Their authority will answer my needs.
Wicked words seem sweet, but they destroy the spirit.
My words seem to stray and tarry, but my spirit, God, is seeking you.
Please keep me from the destitution of a loose tongue.
Let wickedness fall into its own traps, while my spirit makes its escape.

ONE HUNDRED FORTY-TWO

I cry to the Creator, pouring out my complaints, showing my sorrows.
When my spirit is overwhelmed within me,
Only then does the Creator show my path before me.

Ultimately, no person cares for my soul.
They do not fully know me,
Nor can they protect me from the tragedies of living.
Only the Creator rests beyond tragedy, and knows my path through despair.

Creator, attend to my cry.
For I am depressed, and feel persecuted by people and events.
Bring my spirit out of its prisons:
May sincerity encompass me, and my voice risk your glory.
For life remains a bountiful harvest even with its sorrows.

ONE HUNDRED FORTY-THREE

When I am faithful to you, give ear to my hopes.
Do not judge me by your standards, for they are beyond me.
I am persecuted and knocked down by my days.
Darkness pervades my mind. My soul is that of the dead.
My spirit is overwhelmed; my heart is desolate.

I remember better days: seeking your spirit within me,
Becoming absorbed in creation.
I seek you like a desert tree thirsts for water.
Cause me to hear again the bird calls of your love in the morning.
For I still trust life.
Help me to know my way, and to lift up my soul.
Deliver me from my darkness and despair. Teach me to do your will.
The spirit is good, uprightness is still possible,
But I need, quickly, to bring my soul out of trouble.
I would do your will, but I am afflicted.

ONE HUNDRED FORTY-FOUR

It is Creation we should trust. God's spirit is in the courage of our convictions,
In our will to surmount the difficulties of life.
We should wonder at the world's purposes, and question our own importance.
For people are vain, like passing shadows, while the world endures.
Creation breaks forth with mountains and sky.

Deliver us from ourselves, for we are strange children of life.
Our words so often vain, our actions artificial and false,
While we could be singing psalms and playing music.
Rid us of the strange children of our minds,
The forsaken cities of our deeds and dreams,
Deliver us from vanity and falsehood.

Happy are people who reflect the Creation in their lives.
Their sons may grow up like young trees,
Their daughters stand as beautiful and strong as pillars.
For their souls are filled with memories of beauty,
And their minds overflow with deeds of goodness and truth.
Reflecting the Creation, their bodies are strong with generosity,
Their voices ringing with love, and melodic with patience.

Mount McKinley:
Alaska

ONE HUNDRED FORTY-FIVE

The Creator's greatness is unfathomable: incredible works and terrible acts,
Great goodness and stark righteousness.
Yet, the Creator is gracious, and full of compassion,
Slow to anger, and of great mercy. The cosmos will endure.

Creation cushions our falls, evolves our failures into purposes.
Gives each the nourishment of their work in due season,
Satisfies some desires of every living thing.
Creation's way is reality.
Creation's works are the truth.
If you do perceive reality and practice the truth, the Creator will be with you.

ONE HUNDRED FORTY-SIX

Praise God, O my soul.
May I judge life with favor while I have being,
Neither putting all my trust in any leader's hands,
Nor leaning too heavily upon the staff of friendship.
People respond first to their own needs,
And crisis may change any mind in a moment.
Happiness comes to her who wrestles vigorously with her God,
Happiness comes to him who dialogues with his soul,
Hoping to remain afloat upon the rivers of goodness.

We try to be compatible with the Creation
And in alliance with the powers bringing mercy to the oppressed,
And food for the hungry.
We are not meant to be jailers or executioners.
We are not meant even to be disinterested by-standers.
We are meant to help our companions follow the truths of life.

The inner light of the soul, the holy spirit of life,
Can open the eyes of those blind to goodness,
And raise up the heads of those caught in despair.
God loves those with the courage of their own good feelings.
Our tests are with the stranger, the needy, and the oppressed.
Wickedness can turn us all upside down,
But truth will endure, even though we perish.
Praise God, O my soul.

ONE HUNDRED FORTY-SEVEN

Praise gives pleasure to the praised and beauty to their singers.
Communities endure because they gather up outcasts and give them homes.
Thus, does God heal the broken in heart,
Binding up their wounds with human warmth.
Reality confronts us with numbers, names,
And power beyond our understanding.
Often, the hearts of the meek are lifted up,
And the ambitions of the wicked are put aside.
We can all give thanks.

It is fragile clouds that fill the heavens, gentle rain that wears away the stones.
Grass grows up the mountains of every continent.
Even the tiniest beast eats, and few youngsters cry in vain.
Might is not right.
Reason, wonder, and hope are the currency of the faithful.
With these, praise may be given with joy, and received with honor.

If you will attempt lives of goodness the chances of justice are increased.
Creation will give you a peace within your boundaries,
And fill you with more nourishment than can be savored.
See the world, the judgements of nature and the laws of people.
Build up your communities,
Tend the wounds of life with human warmth,
Give and receive the blessings of praise.

ONE HUNDRED FORTY-EIGHT

Praise the Creator beyond the depths and heights your hearts now reach.
Your host upon the Earth, the sun's fire, the stars' light.
A universe unbounded even by the cosmic heavens,
Above the flowing gases, even before time itself.

Praise the Creator.
All things are Its intention.
It is the creative energies themselves,
Nor energy alone, but order too, the natural order,
Evolution evolving on itself.

Praise the Creator, even in the terror and the darkness.
Storms have their beauty, winds their helpfulness.
Embrace the mountains, climb your rugged hills.
Accept the trees of season, and accept the evergreens,
Accept wild beasts, as well as cattle, the myriad insects,
The warbling flocks of birds.
Each is a child of Earth.
All judge their own lives.
Young and old, maiden, ancient man, and child prize the meaning of life.

Praise the Creator before and beyond all possessions.
Creation exalts us.
We reflect Creation in our deeds of generosity and power.
Even we, and our children, are part of Creation.
Praise the Creator.

ONE HUNDRED FORTY-NINE

Sing to God a new song.
Let people rejoice in creation and be happy about their days.
Let them dance and sing in celebration
For God receives energy through the people's joy,
As beauty grows by the people's patient moderation, and gentle goodwill.
Each person can add to the energies of God.

Each person can rise in the morning from sleep into song.
Live with love in your mouth, and reason and justice in your hands.
Share truth with the ignorant, use fairness to confront evil.
Constrain the arrogant, and tax those with unearned pride.
Live with all people a life of reason and justice, a life based on love.
Sing to God a new song.

ONE HUNDRED FIFTY

Twang the harps of life until they sing.
Celebrate in the temples.
Make temples of the streets and workshops of your world.
Grapple gratefully with the powers of Earth.
Prize both the mighty acts and the exquisite details,
The cosmic energies and microscopic orders.
Use every sense and all the body's will,
Use every healthy instrument and reasonable method,
To magnify and glorify the world's essential meaning.
Dance well the beauties of existence.
Think clearly through the symbols of the human quest.
Let everyone that has breath, praise.
Twang the harps of life until they sing.

Musicians:
Stockholm, Sweden

74

ABOUT THE AUTHOR

John Young is a pastor, poet, activist, professor, and author. He was raised in Kansas, earned his doctorate, and was awarded a fellowship at Harvard University. He served congregations in Chicago, New York City, Indiana, New Jersey, California, and is now the Senior Minister at the Unitarian Universalist Church of Jacksonville, Florida, and an Adjunct Professor at the University of North Florida in the Philosophy Department. He recently taught a course on the truth and reconciliation process with Archbishop Desmond Tutu. He has worked on a range of national and international social issues including civil rights, anti-racism, the homeless, world ecumenical understanding, Habitat for Humanity, peace, and disarmament. He has traveled throughout the world, and done research in India and Japan. He is blessed with a gracious wife, Kathleen Moran, and two young adult children, Rahul and Leela Young, who are working to make the world a better place. This book is dedicated to them, and to his parents, Ruth and Cy Young.

Printed in the United States
by Baker & Taylor Publisher Services